CW00542642

A MADE BY BRICK PRODUCTION AT HAMPSTEAD DOWNSTAIRS

# RESPONSIBLE OTHER

## BY MELANIE SPENCER

First performed at Hampstead Theatre,
Downstairs on 20 June 2013

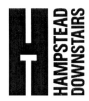

Made By Brick create work that explores modern life. We produce undiscovered British playwrights and striking international writers, connecting theatre audiences with exceptional stories.

We seek to stage contemporary voices that are normally overlooked and have a proven commitment to engaging those who don't normally access the arts.

*Responsible Other* was written by Melanie Spencer (Artistic Director, MBB) in consultation with staff and patients at the Lupus Unit at St Thomas' Hospital. It was long-listed for the Manchester Royal Exchange Bruntwood Prize in 2011.

*Responsible Other* was supported by Guys & St Thomas' Charity, Breathe AHR, Wellcome Trust and Arts Council England.

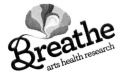

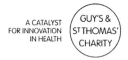

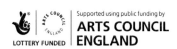

# THANKS

Melanie would particularly like to thank Yvonne Farquharson for taking a chance on her. Also thanks to Tom Hunsinger, Christopher Haydon and Mick Gordon for their faith and encouragement.

Made By Brick would especially like to thank Lynne Kirwin, Beverley Hunt and Steve Winter for their tireless support. Also thanks to all the lupus patients and their relatives at various stages of the process.

The company would also like to thank the following:

Irene Spencer, David Spencer, Susan Forfar, Michael Walters, Daniel O'Connor, Alex Kouzarides, the O'Connor family, the Brockman family, the Templeman family, Imogen Gordon, Angie Davidson, Guys & St Thomas' Charity, Breathe AHR, Wellcome Trust, Arts Council England, The Kevin Spacey Foundation, Old Vic New Voices, The Mackintosh Foundation, Lion Capital, Graham Hughes, Sandy Hampson, Myles Lewis, Louise Nel, Kate Hindle, Timothy Vyse, Cliona Roberts, Elizabeth Lynch, Martine Jean-Baptiste, Miriam Green, Vicky Richardson, Suhayla El-Bushra, Rupert Rowbotham, Gary Lineker, Miranda Bryant, Helen Grady, Georgina Beedle, Andy Rush, Stephanie Fayerman, Katie Lamb, Rebecca Hinds, Grant Gillespie, Debra Baker, Will Rastall, Geoff Breton, Matt Jessup, Sophie Steer, Joseph Wells Wilde, Lookman Sanusi, Moji Bamtefa, Chris Smyrnios, Susie Savafi, Kath Serkis, Jeremy Mortimer, Matt Sedmak, Sue Dunderdale, Andrew Visnevski, Alan Read, Rachael Williams, Lucy Oliver-Harrison, Ebbie McGilp, Hermione Hardwick, Joe Asher, Matt Noddings, Lisa Cagnacci, Zahid Warley, Joe Warley, Kate Holt, Donmar Warehouse, Gate, Bush Theatre, Young Vic and Fortismere School.

Special thanks to all at Oberon Books and Will Mortimer, Becky Paris and the Hampstead Theatre team.

## CAST IN ORDER OF APPEARANCE

**Daisy – Alice Sykes**
**Theatre** credits include *Polar Bears* (Donmar Warehouse) and *Misterman* (Galway Arts Festival/National Theatre).
**Television** credits include *Mad Dogs, Holby City, Midsomer Murders, Postcode, Vera* and *Criminal Justice.*

**Peter – Andy Frame**
**Theatre** credits include *This House, Market Boy, Royal Hunt of the Sun* (National Theatre), *66 Books* (The Bush Theatre), *Wittenberg* (Gate Theatre), *Voyage Round My Father* and *The Winslow Boy* (Salisbury Playhouse), *Six Characters In Search of An Author, Rough Crossings* and *The English Game* (Headlong), *Blue On Blue* (Basingstoke Haymarket Theatre), *Dead Funny* (West Yorkshire Playhouse), *Othello Landscape* (Seinendan, Tokyo), *Festen* (Lyric Theatre), *The Crucible* (Sheffield Crucible Theatre), *All My Sons* (York Theatre Royal), *While I Was Waiting* (BAC), *Marnie-Chester Gateway* (Basingstoke Haymarket), *Romeo and Juliet* (Leicester Haymarket), *Strike Gently, Away From The Body* (Young Vic) and *Small Craft Warnings* (London Pleasance Theatre).
**Television** credits include *Inspector George Gently, EastEnders, Doctors, Silk* and *Holby City* (BBC), *The Bill* (Talkback Thames), *Trial & Retribution* (La Plante Productions), and *Murder Prevention* (Channel 5).
**Film** credits include *Broken* (Cuba Pictures/BBC Films).
**Radio** credits include *Is He Still Breathing?, Life Together* and *Festen* (BBC).

**Alice – Candassaie Liburd**
**Theatre** credits include *Baby Girl* (National Theatre) and *The Tropicali* (Hampstead Theatre). **Television** credits include *Casualty, Perfect Parents* and *The Bill.*
**Film** credits include *Valley of Children.*
**Radio** credits include *8 Feet High and Rising* and *The Lady of Kingsland Waste* (BBC Radio 3).

## Diane – Tricia Kelly

**Theatre** credits include *Cannibals, The Gatekeeper* (Royal Exchange), *The Kitchen* (National Theatre), *Uncle Vanya* (Arcola Theatre/Belgrade), *Tiger Country, The Maths Tutor* (Hampstead Theatre), *Pieces of Vincent* (Arcola), *This Wide Night* (Bernie Grant), *Blue Heaven* (Finborough), *When We Are Married* (West Yorkshire/Liverpool Playhouse), *The Adventures of Nicholas Nickleby* (Gielgud/Chichester/Toronto), *Unprotected* (Everyman Theatre/Traverse), *Some Explicit Polaroids* (Out Of Joint – UK & US tour), *Ion, Julius Caesar* (RSC), *Inland Sea* (Oxford Stage Company/Wilton's Music Hall), *Local* (Royal Court Theatre Upstairs), *A Wife Without a Smile, The House Among the Stars, The Cassilis Engagement, The Way of The World, The Choice* (Orange Tree), *The Seagull, The Government Inspector, As You Like It* (Sheffield Crucible), *Barbarians, Dancing at Lughnasa, Jamaica Inn* (Salisbury), *Season's Greetings, A Whisper of Angel's Wings, Julius Caesar* (Birmingham Rep), *King Lear, Not I, Two, Sunsets & Glories* (West Yorkshire Playhouse), *The Voysey Inheritance* (Edinburgh Lyceum), *Amphytryon* (Gate), *Venus & Lucrece* (Almeida), *Victory* (Wrestling School/Greenwich), *Seven Lears, Golgo, The Last Supper* (Wrestling School/Royal Court Theatre), *Fen* (also New York), *A Mouthful of Birds, Deadlines* (Joint Stock/Royal Court), *The Country Wife, Just Between Ourselves* (Belgrade) and *Saturday Night & Sunday Morning* (Nottingham Playhouse).
**Television and Film** credits include *EastEnders, My Family, Casualty, The Bill, High Stakes, In Sickness and In Health, It's History, Gran, Christobel, Dangerous Lady, A Small Dance, Top Dog* and *Real Lies*.
**Radio** credits include *Pilgrim, St Brice's Day, A Year and a Day* and *Kes*.


## Bola – Yetunde Oduwole

**Theatre** credits include *Pandora's Box* (Arcola Theatre), *The New Boss* (Broadway Theatre), *Torn* (Arcola Theatre), *Wedlock of the Gods* (Cochrane Theatre), *Tiata Delights* (Tiata Fahodzi/Soho Theatre) and *Church* (National Theatre Studio).
**Television** credits include Comfort in E4 series *Youngers* and *Meet The Adebanjos*.
**Film** credits include *Sahara* (Paramount Pictures).

**Miss Lewis – Danielle Bux**

**Theatre** credits include *Calendar Girls* (UK Tour).

**Television** credits include *Silent Witness* (BBC).

**Film** credits include *One Thing Left To Do* (Shane Sweeney), *We Are The Freaks* (104 Films), *DB Shorts* (Clever Boy Media), *Lakeland Falls* (Eye Cue) and *Two Dancers* (James Gardner).

## CREATIVE AND PRODUCTION TEAM FOR MADE BY BRICK

### Director – Melanie Spencer
Melanie studied BA English Literature at University of East Anglia and holds an MA in Text and Performance with Distinction from RADA and Kings College. She is Director of Made By Brick and is Creative Associate at the Gate, former Associate Artist at Southwark Playhouse and was Resident Assistant Director at HighTide 2012-2013. She was part of Chichester Festival Theatre's Young Play-wrights scheme from 2009-2011.

**As Director** credits include *Chicken* (Made By Brick/Southwark Playhouse), *Sense* (Made By Brick/Hen & Chickens), *Honest* (Made By Brick/George Tavern), *White Day* (All The Pigs/New Diorama) and *Neighbors* (HighTide (2012)/Public Theater, New York).

**As Assistant Director** credits include *The Promise* (Donmar Trafalgar), *Sunset Baby* and *Wittenberg* (Gate), *Boys* (Headlong/HighTide), *Souvenirs* (Tamasha) and *Bea* (On Theatre).

### Producer – Clemmie Forfar
Clemmie studied BA English Literature and Drama at the University of East Anglia. She is Producer of Made By Brick and is Associate Producer at The Yard and Urgent Theatre.

**As Producer** credits include *The Generation Game* (The Yard), *The Hospital At The Time Of The Revolution* (The Finborough), The 24 Hour Plays, The 24 Hour Musicals (The Old Vic), *Honest* (Made By Brick/George Tavern), *Sense* (Made By Brick/Hen & Chickens) and *Chicken* (Made By Brick/Southwark Playhouse).

### Design – Emma Tompkins
Emma studied at Nottingham Trent. Emma is a previous recipient of the No Stirngs Attached Grant from the Farnham Maltings and the Incubate scheme at The Little Angel Theatre in support of her puppetry production with Jenkins Ait.

**As Designer** credits include *The Story of the Four Children Who Went Round the World* (tour), *A Broken Rose* (Cockpit Theatre), *King John* (Union Theatre), *Sense* (Hens and Chickens), *The Price of Everything* (National Tour), *The Lonely Hearts Comedy Club* (The Old Vic Tunnels, Stockholm) and *3P/Bronwen Carr* (Network Theatre).

**As Associate Designer** credits include *Wittenberg* (The Gate), *Double Falsehood* and *Fing's Aint What They Used t'be* (The Steam Industry) and *Mokitagrit* (Union Theatre).

**Sound – Tom Hackley**

Tom studied BA Theatre Sound at CSSD.

**Sound Designs** include *Trial of Ubu* and *Say it with Flowers* (Hampstead), *Bowl Of Cherries* (Charring Cross), *Clemency* and *Isola Disabitata* (Royal Opera House), *Haunting Julia* (UK Tour/ Riverside Studio), *The Baroque Story* and *A Little Neck* (Hampton Court), *Burning Gardens, Lost Fortune, One For Sorrow, Fool's Gold, Oedipus, Masks, Warnings, Child of Chance, The Knucker, Strippers & Gentlemen, Pelléas and Mélisande* (Found Space), *Fragments* (E.N.O.), *Early Days* (National Theatre (Wales)), *Novero* (Red Dot, Essen), *Jesus Hopped the A Train* (Trafalgar Studios), *A Man of No Importance* and *Saturday Night* (Arts Theatre), *Monsters, Miracle* and *Exotic Tastes* (Arcola), *603 Reading* (Royal Court), *Senora Carrar's rifles* and *Pope's Wedding* (Young Vic), *Doubt: a parable* and *To Kill A Mockingbird* (Tricycle) and *Silence Is Golden* [Film] (B.F.I.).

**Production Sound** credits also include work for National Theatre, Lyric & Hammersmith, Sadler's Wells, The Place, Queen's Theatre, Old Vic, Jasmin Vardimon, Goat & Monkey, CPA, Complicite, The Comedy Theatre, The Bush Theatre, Gate Theatre, Mela Festival, IF Festival, Old Vic Tunnels, Lovebox, Somerset House, Isle of White Festival and Alexandra Palace.


**Dramaturge – Rob Drummer**

Rob is Associate Dramaturge at The Bush Theatre, previously he was the first Literary Manager and principle Dramaturge at HighTide Festival Theatre.

**As Dramaturge** credits include *Home* (National Theatre), *Bottleneck* (HighTide/Soho), *Mudlarks* (HighTide/Bush Theatre), *Organs of Little Apparent Importance* (HighTide).

**As Director** credits include *Sense* (Company of Angels), *Endless Poem* (HighTide/People's Palace Projects/London 2012 Festival), *Eisteddfod* (HighTide/Latitude), *Perish* (HighTide/Public Theater, New York), *Flora* (Theatre503), *Baggage* (Horseplay Arts Club), *People You May Know* (York Theatre Royal), *Whose Cloud is it Anyway?* (People Show Studios), *A Girl in a Car With a Man* (Contact) and *The Yellow Wallpaper* (Manchester Museum).

**As Assistant Director** credits include *The Train Driver* (Hampstead Theatre), *Dusk Rings a Bell* and *Incoming* (HighTide).

**Lighting – Katherine Graham**

Katherine studied at Trinity College, Dublin and has an MA in Visual Language of Performance from Wimbledon College of Art. Lighting Design credits include *Sense* and *Chicken* (Made by Brick), *The Little Soldiers* (Theatre Re, Cockpit Theatre), *Nineveh* (Theatre Temoin, Riverside Studios), *Sleeping Beauty* (The Castle, Wellingborough), *BYPASS* (Painted Filly, Dublin), *The Gambler* (Theatre Re), *The Bright Side of the Moon* (Beyond the Bark, *You Can't Just Leave ... There's Always Something, Andy Warhol's Nothing Special* and *Soh* (all with Split Gin), *Don Juan in Hell* (Belltable, Limerick), *The Butcher Babes* (The New Theatre, Dublin), *Through a Film Darkly* (Project, Dublin), *The Trials of Brother Jero* and *Pantomime* (Arambe), *Masse Mench* (Volksbühne, Berlin), *Art* (Mephisto), *You Wish!* (Riverbank), *The Cabinet of Dr Caligari* (Samuel Beckett Theatre), *Waiting for Godot* (AC Productions). Stage and Lighting design for *Cinderella, Romeo and Juliet* (both with Ballet Ireland), *The Common Will* and *100 Minutes* (both with Painted Filly).

Other work includes immersive installations *Re-membering* (Wimbledon), *Hiding / Seeking* (Performance Space, Hackney) and the international walking art project *A City Walk*.

**Costume Supervisor – Natasha Mackmurdie**

Natasha studied BA Costume Design and Technical Arts for Performance at London College of Fashion.

**Costume Supervisor** credits include *Aida* (ROH), *Cinderella* (EN), *A Midsummer Night's Dream* (NB), *Fancy Free* (BRB), *The Rover* (Hampton Court Palace), *Broken Rose* (Cockpit Theatre), *Yerma, An Absolute Turkey* (East 15), *A Holding Space* (Dance United). *The Parades Gone By* (Ballet Rambert), *Stephen and the Sexy Partridge* (Red Lion Theatre), *Sense* (Hen and Chickens Theatre), *Last Days of Judas Iscariot* (Lewisham College), *King John* (Union Theatre), *Sleeping Beauty* (Woodville Hall), *Peter Pan* (Gracie Fields Hall), *Bella Époque* (Park Lane), *Onegin* (Bury Court Opera), *West Side Story* (NYMT), *Salome, Barbarians, Balm in Gilead, Random Acts of Kindness, Don Juan on Trial, All that Falls, Brother Size, The Rivals, Loyal Women, Reigen, The Cosmonaut's Last Message from the USSR, Vassa, Fanny's First Play, Touched, Three Sisters, Wuthering Heights, Hiawatha, Oh! What a Lovely War, Canterbury Tales, Much Ado About Nothing, Romeo and Juliet* (Royal Academy of Dramatic Art).

**Filming** credits include *Fire, On this island, Shadow Boxer, King John, Scene Five* (Short films), *Anna Karenina* and *The World's End* (Feature films), *Siege of Athlone* and *Dr Tatiana's sex advice to all creation* (Documentary), and *Pumpkin Soup* (Music Video for Kate Nash).

### Production Manager – Ed Wilson

Ed trained at Bretton Hall College.

**Production Management** credits include *Scrooge* (Birmingham Alexandra), *Mojo* and *The Weir* (Royal Court Theatre), *Cleansed, Via Dolorosa* and *The Leenane Trilogy* (West End/Broadway), *The Chairs* (Complicite UK/Broadway) and *Street Of Crocodiles* (Lincoln Centre Festival). Other credits include *As You Like It, A Light In The Piazza* and *Peter Pan* (Curve Leicester), *Romeo and Juliet* (Ludlow Festival), *Dandy In The Underworld* and *Fit and Proper People* (Soho), *Zaide* (Classical Opera Company), *House of Ghosts* (Calibre Productions), *Belongings* (Hampstead Theatre/ Trafalgar Studios), and *Julius Ceasar* (ENO).

Ed has recently Production Managed the European Tour of *The Master and Margarita* for Complicite and also Production Managed for ENO and been Technical Director of the Theatre Royal Plymouth.

Ed has worked in a freelance capacity for Cameron Mackintosh Ltd. Other clients have included WNO, Disney Theatrical/Stage Entertainment, and New Adventures Ltd for *Edward Scissorhands, The Car Man, Nutcracker!* and *Dorian Gray*.

Ed is currently the resident Production Manager of *Billy Elliot* in the West End and is working on *Neville's Island* for Chichester Festival Theatre.

### Assistant Director – Simon Ryninks

Simon studied Drama & Script Writing at the University of East Anglia.

**As Director** (theatre) credits include *O Brave New World* (Create Festival) and *Judgement* (Somerset House).

**As Director** (television) credits include *Jail Tales* and *How Banks Work* (BBC 3).

Simon also directs short films and music videos as part of The Unthank Alliance.

**Assistant Producer – Caggy Kerlogue**
Caggy studied Script Writing & Performance at the University of East Anglia.
**As Assistant Producer** credits include *Honest* (upstairs at The George), *Company, Parade, Victor Victoria* and *Mack and Mabel* (Southwark Playhouse), *Pitchfork Disney* (Arcola), *Burlesque* and *Drowning on Dry Land* (Jermyn Street) and *Noël and Gertie* (Cockpit).

**Deputy Stage Manager – Eleanor Dixon**
Eleanor studied with the Court Theatre Training Company.
**Stage Manager On The Book** credits include *Richard II* and *Comedy Of Errors* (Tobacco Factory Bristol).
**Deputy Stage Manager** credits include *Pericles, Three Sisters, Titus Andronicus, Love's Labour's Lost, Othello, Much Ado About Nothing, Taming of The Shrew, Hamlet, A Midsummer Night's Dream* and *The Tempest* (Tobacco Factory Bristol), *The Good Soldier* and *Herding Cats* (Ustinov Theatre Bath), *65 Miles* and *Once Upon A Time in Wigan* (Hull Truck Theatre Company), *The Glee Club* (Hull Truck and National Tour), *The Misanthrope* (Theatre Royal Bristol), *Uncle Vanya* and *On The Waterfront* (Edinburgh Fringe Festival).
**Assistant Stage Manager** credits include *Peter Pan, Cinderella* and *Sleeping Beauty* (Grand Theatre Blackpool).

**Company Stage Manager – Ella Bolton**
Ella studied Stage Management & Technical Theatre at Guildhall School of Music and Drama.
**Stage Management** credits include *Mydidae* (Trafalgar Studio 2), *Alexei Sayle* and *The Rubberbandits* (Soho Theatre), *The Seagull* (Southwark Playhouse), *The Intervention* (The Comedians Theatre Company) and *Stewart Lee* (Leicester Square Theatre).
**Tour Management** credits include *Michaela Strachan's Really Wild Adventures* (UK Tour), *Simon Amstell* and *Numb* (National Tour).
**DSM** credits include *Queen of Spades* (Arcola Theatre).
**ASM** credits include *Dance Umbrella, Square Dances* and *Gordon Square* (Bloomsbury) and *Oliver!* (Theatre Royal Drury Lane).

# FOREWORD

As an NHS consultant, I've been blessed with some very talented temporary secretaries over the years. The working environment is hectic; multi-tasking and asking for help and advice are a daily norm, often resulting in staff chatting and sharing their stories and ideas. Alongside secretarial work, most of my staff have supported other careers and interests, such as motorcycling and male pole dancing (yes, really!). But none had the intellectual curiosity and intense interest in people that Melanie Spencer showed. Melanie had a fairly long spell working in the Lupus Unit and, after typing up hundreds of my letters from clinic appointments, she became relatively knowledgeable about lupus. Did she simply type the patient letters or had she absorbed the medical information and emotional stories into her own psyche? Both, probably.

Upon meeting Melanie, it was clear that she had the brain, drive and emotional makeup to succeed in the theatre world as both a writer and director. Her commitment to Made By Brick, which she founded with producer Clemmie Forfar, is remarkable. Both are passionate about presenting stories of untold truths that need to be heard; quite daunting really, and enough to make you feel very humble. I advised Melanie to help her write a plausible story about life with a chronic auto-immune disease. If any medics find errors in the script, please blame me, not Melanie, for the medical input is mine.

So what is lupus? Short for systemic lupus erythematosus, it's an auto-immune condition; a state where antibodies – proteins that should fight invading bugs – instead attack and destroy body proteins. It probably affects about one in a thousand people, mainly women, and has many symptoms, the main ones being joint pain, severe fatigue and skin rashes. We call this 'mild' lupus. Not because the symptoms aren't earth-shatteringly awful to the individual but because thankfully these symptoms don't have any long-term harmful effects to the body.

But lupus can cause major harm and as a doctor I'm constantly on the look-out for the first sign of failing kidneys (lupus nephritis). Unchecked, this condition can cause irreparable harm, such that the kidneys fail and dialysis is required to keep the patient alive. In 2013, we would hope patients would be offered a renal transplant before this happened. However, caught early and treated aggressively with powerful drugs such as cyclophosphamide, lupus nephritis can be dampened down and damage prevented altogether. So, why should you know about lupus? Well, you'll probably find that you actually know of someone with it or a similar auto-immune condition.

One of the nightmares of lupus is that it can and does affect young people. It's hard enough to cope with the emotional rollercoaster of being a teenager, let alone carry the burden of a chronic disease as well. *Responsible Other* serves a wider purpose of not just letting you know what lupus is but also exploring the emotional impact of a chronic disease on a teenager and their family.

**Prof Beverley Hunt**

# A PERSONAL ACCOUNT OF LIVING WITH LUPUS

I was diagnosed with Lupus in April 2012. I was sixteen and embarking on my GCSEs. Since January of that year I had been continuously unwell, suffering from painful, raw blisters on the joints in my body. My eyes would swell on random occasions and my skin would become rough, dry and sore. I became extremely tired and weak, not being able to get out of bed. I lost weight and looked and felt dreadful.

The doctors first thought the blisters were due to an allergic reaction and tried treating me with strong antihistamines which didn't work. Eventually, they resorted to prescribing a daily high dose of steroids to help my body take back control. Although the blisters were tempered, I still wasn't myself. Each time I came off the steroids I would become extremely unwell again. My GCSEs were approaching fast and I was missing a lot of school. Finally, I saw a specialist.

It was then that I first heard the word lupus. I was told about its symptoms and its potentially wide-reaching effects on my life – now and in the future. I found the illness very confusing and hard to understand; it can present itself in the form of anything from a cold, to something as serious as organ failure and there is no simple treatment. It was all too hard to accept. I went into denial.

Lupus is difficult to explain and I wasn't able to communicate clearly to others what was wrong with me. My personality changed. I became very tense and snappy with everyone. Mum was determined to make sure I had the best care possible. She contacted people from lupus support groups and even attended an event in Cardiff, meeting with professionals working with lupus sufferers.

I got referred to UCLH (University College London Hospital), Adolescent Rheumatology Department. Unfortunately, I wasn't getting any better and was put on a cocktail of drugs to keep my flares[1] under control. It was tough and the drugs caused distressing side effects such as hair loss. In terms of treatment, as with many lupus patients, it was often a case of trying a variety of drugs and coping mechanisms, to discover what management worked at any given time. In October 2012, I became very unwell again. I was diagnosed with a serious kidney infection and put on yet another course of strong medication.

My school has been very supportive. I got the best help possible for my exams and have achieved brilliant grades. I began to accept the illness and developed the attitude of not letting it stop me in life. I got a Saturday job just like all my friends and worked through the whole summer. I'm currently stable, on a low dose of medication and feel the most like 'me' that I have in a long time. I've learned to adjust, listen to my body and accept that I have a chronic, permanent life-affecting illness. And that's okay.

**Jenny Brockman** (17 years)

---

[1]    'A flare' is the term for an acute period of lupus-related illness.

# RESPONSIBLE OTHER

Melanie Spencer

OBERON BOOKS
LONDON

WWW.OBERONBOOKS.COM

First published in 2013 by Oberon Books Ltd
521 Caledonian Road, London N7 9RH
Tel: +44 (0) 20 7607 3637 / Fax: +44 (0) 20 7607 3629
e-mail: info@oberonbooks.com
www.oberonbooks.com

A catalogue record for this book is available from the British
Library.

PB ISBN: 978-1-78319-026-3
E ISBN: 978-1-78319-525-1

Cover design by James Illman

Printed, bound and converted
by CPI Group (UK) Ltd, Croydon, CR0 4YY.

Visit www.oberonbooks.com to read more about all our books
and to buy them. You will also find features, author interviews and
news of any author events, and you can sign up for e-newsletters
so that you're always first to hear about our new releases.

*For Catherine*

# Characters

DAISY (15)

PETER (early 50s)

DIANE (late 50s)

ALICE (15)

BOLA (Nigerian, 30s – 40s)

MISS LEWIS (30s)

# ONE

*PETER's sitting room.*

*DAISY is lying on the sofa under a duvet. A laptop is open next to her. The television is on. She is taking selfies on her mobile phone, contorting her face into silly expressions.*

*A half-eaten plate of biscuits and other debris surrounds the sofa. There are several discarded gossip magazines on the floor. There is one broadsheet newspaper, crisp and unopened on the coffee table.*

*The house phone rings. DAISY appears oblivious. Her mobile phone rings, playing something inane and current. She dances along before she answers.*

DAISY:      What?

            Yes. Fine.

            No.

            I've done a bit.

            I have! I am doing something useful! Why do you always ask me that?

            So why are you ringing me if you're outside, you loser?!

            Bye! *BYE!*

            *DAISY hangs up and chucks the phone absent-mindedly. PETER enters angrily wearing a suit, tie and carrying a briefcase.*

PETER:      Do not speak to me like that.

DAISY:      Sorry.

PETER:      Particularly don't speak to me like that and then hang up.

DAISY:      Sorry.

PETER:      How dare you call me a loser. What do you think you're playing at?

DAISY:      Nothing.

PETER:      It's verbal abuse, Daisy.

DAISY:      As if it is!

23

| | |
|---|---|
| PETER: | It's not on. |
| DAISY: | I was *joking*! It was a joke. *Joke.* Ha *ha.* Fun-*nee.* |
| PETER: | Why are you not dressed? |
| DAISY: | I wasn't going anywhere. |
| PETER: | Daisy, I really think… You know: it's actually psychologically important to – |
| DAISY: | I wasn't going anywhere, was I? |
| PETER: | Don't interrupt me Daisy, please. |
| DAISY: | For God's sake. |
| PETER: | Getting dressed is hardly. You know. Labour intensive. |
| DAISY: | – |
| PETER: | Is it? |
| DAISY: | What more proof do you need? Seriously. |
| PETER: | Don't say that so – |
| DAISY: | 'So' what? |
| PETER: | Flippantly. |
| DAISY: | Why? |
| PETER: | Just. Just don't. |

*PETER removes jacket, shoes, tie. DAISY turns her attention to 'Hollyoaks' by putting the sound up.*

Any phone calls?

Er. Hello?

*DAISY turns the sound down.*

| | |
|---|---|
| DAISY: | What now? I'm on my lunch break. |
| PETER: | Is this you still joking? |
| DAISY: | Yes. It's, like, six o'clock, Dad. |
| PETER: | Did anyone call? |
| DAISY: | Were you expecting a call? |
| PETER: | Well… The hospital? |

DAISY:      It rang, like, two times or something.

PETER:      And? Who was it?

DAISY:      Some robot. 'Have *you* had an accident at work?'

PETER:      What is this? *(Pointing at television.)*

DAISY:      Trash.

PETER:      What trash?

DAISY:      *Hollyoaks.*

PETER:      So. Who's the one with the eyebrows?

DAISY:      She's a pregnant chav.

PETER:      Chav.

DAISY:      Yes.

PETER:      You're not a chav, are you?

DAISY:      No. I'm just pregnant.

PETER:      Read the paper?

DAISY:      Not yet.

PETER:      Ok.

DAISY:      Don't say it.

PETER:      I just said 'Ok.'

DAISY:      Don't.

PETER:      I didn't say anything.

DAISY:      'You're a day behind the rest of the world.'

PETER:      You are.

            *PETER looks at the magazines on the floor.*

            This looks informative.

DAISY:      Alice brought them.

PETER:      Oh. R-Patz has split up with K-Stew.

DAISY:      I told you. Alice brought them.

PETER:      There's a flood in Pakistan. Did you know that?

DAISY:      For the last time: Alice. Brought. Them.

PETER:     A likely story.

DAISY:     Well, it's not like *I* went to the shop, is it?

PETER:     Are we watching this? *(Pointing to television.)*

DAISY:     *I'm* trying to. But *we're* talking. So I've turned the sound down.

PETER:     Well, if we're not definitively *watching* it, let's turn it *off* altogether for the moment and think of the planet.

DAISY:     Who always forgets to put out the recycling?

PETER:     Daisy –

DAISY:     Not me, is it?

PETER:     Daisy. Not a *day* goes by in this house when I do not turn an unnecessary light *off*.

DAISY:     Don't start talking about compost.

PETER:     Every room like the Blackpool illuminations. Everything bip-bipping away on standby.

DAISY:     I'll scream if you talk about the compost bin. I mean it.

PETER:     Look. The compost bin –

DAISY:     Dad! I cannot talk to you about compost anymore! Alright?! I'm seriously sick of it!

           *DAISY turns the television off.*

           OFF!

PETER:     Thank you.

           So.

           Did Alice bring any schoolwork?

DAISY:     Worksheets.

PETER:     What worksheets?

DAISY:     Worksheets. Shit like that.

PETER:     Yes but *what* worksheets? What subjects?

DAISY:     I don't know. Maths!

PETER: Daisy, I would be very grateful if you would please just answer my very straightforward and reasonable questions, ok, in a civil manner; no swearing and without behaving all…'kicking to the curb' or whatever it is you're doing. It's boring.

DAISY: Go on then. Ask.

PETER: Did you add the worksheets to the homework chart?

DAISY: Yes.

PETER: Right. That was all I needed to know.

I do have a day job as well as being your homework manager.

DAISY: Brownian motion. Go on. Ask me a question about that.

PETER: Ok. Er.

DAISY: Because I did do a bit of Physics earlier.

PETER: Good.

DAISY: Look. The revision guide.

PETER: Good. I'm pleased.

DAISY: –

PETER: Now.

I checked the train times for Friday.

DAISY: I don't want to talk about it.

PETER: We have to talk about it.

DAISY: We don't have to talk about it *this second*.

PETER: It would make me feel better.

DAISY: –

PETER: The appointment is nine. If we catch the seven thirteen –

DAISY: Oh my God.

PETER: We will arrive in London at eleven minutes past eight. That gives us almost an hour to get to Westminster.

DAISY: So.

PETER: So. Factoring in the drive to the station. Set your alarm for ten to six. I want to be on the safe side. Ok?

DAISY: Ok.

PETER: Hey.

DAISY: –

PETER: I said, hey.

DAISY: Hi.

PETER: This is normal.

DAISY: No it's not.

PETER: No. It's not. But that's not what I meant. I meant you being horrid to me is normal.

DAISY: –

PETER: Makes it easier for us to separate. Apparently. I read about it in a parenting…thing.

DAISY: What 'parenting' thing?

PETER: An article about teenagers. Sheree gave me it.

DAISY: Who's Sheree?

PETER: Who's Sheree. Sheree is a very nice lady who I have known for many years. Part of the Birmingham sales team.

DAISY: She better be a minger.

PETER: She's married, in her sixties and has two grown-up sons.

DAISY: Good.

PETER: –

DAISY: –

| | |
|---|---|
| PETER: | Oh for God's Sake. Switch it back on. We'll pretend I never saw. |
| DAISY: | I don't like *Hollyoaks*, Dad. |
| PETER: | Ok, Daisy. |
| | *PETER exits.* |
| DAISY: | I don't. It's just always on. |

## TWO

*PETER and DAISY's living room.*

*ALICE has let herself in. She is wearing school uniform. DAISY appears to be asleep.*

| | |
|---|---|
| ALICE: | Hi! |
| | I got a new keyring. |
| | It's a polar bear. |
| DAISY: | You have a keyring addiction. |
| ALICE: | Why are you always asleep when I get here? |
| DAISY: | I'm not. |
| ALICE: | Some of us have been at school all day. |
| | Slaving away. At school. You know? *School.* |
| | Hiya. |
| DAISY: | Hi. |
| ALICE: | What did you dream about? |
| DAISY: | Nothing. |
| ALICE: | Mr Phillips? |
| DAISY: | No. |
| ALICE: | But you *did*, didn't you? |
| DAISY: | *No.* |
| ALICE: | You had sex with Mr Phillips in your dream didn't you? |
| DAISY: | No! |

| | |
|---|---|
| ALICE: | OMG. You literally did have sex with him in your dream though, didn't you? |
| DAISY: | Don't make me *chunder*, Alice. He's rotten. And married. |

*ALICE eats a biscuit.*

| | |
|---|---|
| ALICE: | I turn into a right diva when I'm hungry. |
| DAISY: | I thought your mum had you on a diet? |
| ALICE: | Are you saying I'm chunks? |
| DAISY: | No! |
| ALICE: | I am really fat though. No! I am! I know I am. |
| DAISY: | You're not. |
| ALICE: | Trying not to eat breakfast. |
| DAISY: | Alice. |
| ALICE: | Only had a packet of Chipsticks for lunch. |
| DAISY: | They're crisps. |
| ALICE: | Yeah but they are literally sticks of air. You can't survive on them. |
| DAISY: | You're not fat. |
| ALICE: | I've been starving all day, so it's working. |
| DAISY: | You're not fat! |
| ALICE: | Phase two is to hopefully catch bulimia before Normandy. But definitely before One Direction at the 02. |
| DAISY: | You can't catch bulimia, you idiot! |

*ALICE whips out a load of worksheets that are crushed and dog-eared from her bag.*

| | |
|---|---|
| | Letter. About Normandy. |
| DAISY: | Thanks. |
| | I still don't know yet. |

ALICE: But Daisy I need to sort out my dormitory! I'll be put with the losers! I'll have to go around the whole of France by myself!

DAISY: You won't.

ALICE: I'll have to sit with the teachers on the coach!

DAISY: You won't!

ALICE: I really will!

DAISY: You won't.

ALICE: When will you know?

DAISY: I don't know. Soon.

ALICE: Tell your dad it's a big deal. We've been planning it since Year Seven.

DAISY: Alice. It's not like I don't want to go. I want to go.

ALICE: I know you said there isn't a cure. But science will find a cure. You just got to keep positive and everything.

DAISY: Thanks.

ALICE: Hey. I'd give wifey my kidney. If my mum let me.

DAISY: Thanks.

ALICE: Homework.

DAISY: What is it?

ALICE: French. Le camping.

DAISY: Eurgh. C'est *bof.*

ALICE: No. You're so crappy at impressions. Got to say it like you're going to literally be sick.

Sest BOF.

DAISY: *BOFFFF.*

ALICE: More burpy. BOEUFFFF.

DAISY: –

ALICE: Well. I am the ultimate champion.

Shall I add this to your homework chart?

DAISY: Nah. Talk to me. Tell me something funny.

ALICE: Um. I got bored and drew loads of stuff on my textbook.

DAISY: Like what?

ALICE: Um. A couple of willies. Some devil horns.

DAISY: Standard.

ALICE: But then everyone had to get into pairs. And I had to be partners with Miss. She was all jibber jabber in French. I had to sit with my arm weird – like this. I couldn't concentrate. I was so stressed out in case she saw them devils. Shit would have gone down.

DAISY: That's not funny.

ALICE: Hey. It is a bit funny.

DAISY: Talking about French twenty-four seven does not mean I can go to Normandy.

ALICE: Well: I've got better news. Big, big, big news. Out of school big, big news. But I won't tell you if you're going to be a biatch.

*ALICE has retrieved a bag of Chipsticks from her schoolbag, which she now eats triumphantly.*

DAISY: You can't leave it there! Go on!

ALICE: No. It's too good. And you didn't say anything nice about my keyring.

DAISY: I love your new keyring. I love all your keyrings.

ALICE: No. You'll have to work for it.

DAISY: Tell me!

ALICE: No.

DAISY: Tell me!

ALICE: No.

DAISY: Tell me!

ALICE: Ooo-kay.

*ALICE gives DAISY a scrunched-up piece of paper.*

Wa-la. *('Voilà')*

DAISY:     Wow. A random bit of paper.

ALICE:     It's a Blackberry Messenger Pin.

DAISY:     How useful as I don't have a Blackberry.

ALICE:     Nah but it's like important. An important person.

DAISY:     Who?

ALICE:     You're going to love me so much.

DAISY:     Who?

ALICE:     Think.

DAISY:     I don't believe you.

ALICE:     Yep.

DAISY:     No.

ALICE:     Honestly.

DAISY:     Fuck.

ALICE:     His real name's Kyle.

DAISY:     Really?!

ALICE:     *Yep*.

DAISY:     He looks like a Kyle. Doesn't he?

ALICE:     I know.

DAISY:     How did you find out?

ALICE:     Top secret.

DAISY:     Alice!

ALICE:     I have my ways. I did it for you. To cheer you up.

DAISY:     Tell me.

ALICE:     Ok, ok. I walked up to him this morning at the bus stop, yeah: 'We've never met you. So this is crazy. Here's Daisy's number. So call her maybe.'

DAISY:     Oh my God, you didn't.

ALICE:     But I did though.

DAISY:      You didn't. You wouldn't.

ALICE:      So. Ok. So. I went to Vicky's house.

DAISY:      Vicky?!

ALICE:      No. Not that Vicky. She has B.O. No. Other Vicky.

DAISY:      Hold the phone. Vicky *Brampton*.

ALICE:      Yeah.

DAISY:      What the fuck?

ALICE:      That was in Year Seven. She's not like that anymore.

DAISY:      Well. She was still a bitch when I last saw her.

ALICE:      Do you want to hear the story or not?

DAISY:      Yeah. But she is a bitch.

ALICE:      She really isn't Daisy. We're like…we're sort of friends now.

DAISY:      –

ALICE:      Basically. She invited me round to her house.

DAISY:      What?!

ALICE:      I know.

DAISY:      Random.

ALICE:      A bit.

DAISY:      When?!

ALICE:      Saturday.

DAISY:      Why did you not tell me this when you came over on Monday?!

ALICE:      I forgot.

DAISY:      How could you forget that?!

ALICE:      I was in a rush!

DAISY:      Were you?!

ALICE:      Yeah! I do rhythmic gymnastics on Mondays, remember. I had all my kit with me and everything.

DAISY:     Move please. I need to lie down.

ALICE:     Well. Some other people were there. Well. You know, Slutty Ashley and Gemma F.

DAISY:     What did you do?

ALICE:     We sat around really. Watched TV. Went on Chat Roulette. Did a Keek.

DAISY:     You Keeked?

ALICE:     Just one. Look. Let me tell you about Kyle.

So. We were all upstairs drinking Malibu in Vicky's bedroom. And, ok to be fair, slutty Ashley was, y'know, telling everyone her favourite-ever life experience *again*. Blah blah blah – how she got fingered by that thirty-year-old waiter in Tenerife – blah blah blah.

DAISY:     So gross.

ALICE:     *Then* gave him a blow job whilst he sat on a jet ski. Apparently.

DAISY:     That must be a lie.

ALICE:     Then we went on Facebook, right, when all of a sudden *Kyle* popped up in this really hot photograph. So I asked Vicky 'oh, who's that? I *think* he might wait at my bus stop'. And she said 'oh, *Kyle*, he's friends with my big sister. They work at Sainsbury's together'.

DAISY:     Ok.

ALICE:     Um. What else? Oh. He's seventeen.

DAISY:     I *told* you! *I told you* he was older than us.

ALICE:     He's got a baby face!

DAISY:     Doesn't wear a school uniform though does he?

ALICE:     No. Studies BTEC Music. At college.

DAISY:     I *knew* he'd be in a band.

ALICE:     And. His surname's 'Thompson.'

DAISY:     Kyle. Thompson.

ALICE:     Yeah.

DAISY:     Suits him, doesn't it? I really like it.

ALICE:     I want a boyfriend called Theo or Jay.

DAISY:     You didn't tell Vicky about me liking Kyle did you?

ALICE:     No!

           Now. I think you should Snapchat Kyle a picture of your bum.

DAISY:     No!

ALICE:     Your face then!

DAISY:     Hey. Do you remember when you got off with that boy Matt outside McDonald's after knowing him for two hours!

ALICE:     That was in Year Eight! Year *Eight*. At least I've had my first kiss. And my second, third, fourth. *Five* now, actually.

DAISY:     Five?! Who was the fifth?

ALICE:     Doesn't matter.

DAISY:     Secretive.

ALICE:     Hey. Do you remember when your Mum caught us shoplifting Percy Pigs from Marks and Spencer? That was so bad.

DAISY:     What made you bring that up?

ALICE:     Well, that was *classic* Year Eight.

DAISY:     So fucking classic.

ALICE:     I miss you.

DAISY:     You see me all the time.

ALICE:     You know what I mean.

DAISY:     Actually. I might not be in on Friday.

ALICE:     Say what? I thought we were watching *The Hunger Games*?

DAISY:     Something with my dad again.

ALICE:      Oh.

DAISY:      Hospital.

ALICE:      Oh. Oh right…

            At least it's like a London hospital you go to.

DAISY:      What do you mean?

ALICE:      Well. It's like cooler to go to hospital there than, like, here, isn't it? I bet all the other patients are like celebrities or whatever.

DAISY:      I haven't seen anyone famous.

ALICE:      I won't come round on Friday then.

            *Thinks.*

            Do you think I'd pass for eighteen if I wore high heels and loads of make-up?

DAISY:      Dunno. Why?

ALICE:      This will sound weird and embarrassing, right, and I'd only say it to you because you're my best friend and everything.

DAISY:      Yeah.

ALICE:      I need a new coat. And it got me thinking. Who am I? Topshop or Miss Selfridge? Do you know what I mean?

DAISY:      Yeah.

ALICE:      Or H&M.

DAISY:      Or *vintage.*

ALICE:      That's so much effort though isn't it? Where do you go?

DAISY:      Charity shops?

ALICE:      Bleurgh. No way.

            What's your mum's stuff like?

DAISY:      Dunno.

ALICE:      'Dunno.'

DAISY:    As in. I dunno. I haven't seen it. I don't know where it is or whatever.

ALICE:    'Cause, well, you could wear anything you liked of hers now, couldn't you?

DAISY:    I suppose.

ALICE:    You should ask your dad.

DAISY:    Maybe.

ALICE:    Or we could go down London or something. Look for good vintage stuff. I could come with you to the hospital one day. I'd have to go with you or I won't know where I'm going otherwise 'cause it's, like, London. What? Don't you want to?

DAISY:    I do. It's just. I get quite tired.

ALICE:    We could go. Once you're better.

DAISY:    I don't want to talk about it, Alice.

ALICE:    Ok. What should we talk about then?

## THREE

*Outside St Thomas' Hospital. A bench facing Big Ben.*

*PETER has been waiting for DAISY for quite a while. He holds two styrofoam cups of something hot and disappointing.*

*DAISY appears. She is wearing heart sunglasses, a cat hat, kitten mittens and a winter coat.*

PETER:    Hi.

You were a long time.

Do you… Do you have a poorly tummy?

DAISY:    Oh my God, Dad. Don't ask me that!! How embarrassing! Jesus.

PETER:    I've been admiring Big Ben. Whilst you were… wherever you've just been for half an hour.

Weird. Isn't it? There's Big Ben.

PETER:    Where have you been?

DAISY:      Nowhere.

PETER:      So why were you there so long?

            You didn't answer your phone.

            I didn't know. What to think.

DAISY:      I just wanted a moment to myself. It's not illegal.

PETER:      Oh. Ok. Whatever, whatever.

DAISY:      –

PETER:      Tea.

DAISY:      I don't want it.

PETER:      It'll warm your hands.

            *DAISY lifts up her hands, which are dressed as two cats.*

DAISY:      I've got the kitten mittens.

            *She gestures to her hat.*

            And the cat hat.

PETER:      I know, Daisy. But it's freezing out here.

DAISY:      It's not. It's 'fresh.'

PETER:      Don't get smart.

DAISY:      That's what *she* would've said.

PETER:      Oh. Sorry.

DAISY:      You always jump down my throat, Dad.

PETER:      Sorry.

            It is fresh. Yes.

            Have you got enough suncream on?

DAISY:      Got my sunglasses on. Got shitloads of suncream
            on. Just. Chillax.

PETER:      I really wish you'd drink the tea.

DAISY:      Why?

PETER:      It cost me two pounds seventy.

            *DAISY takes the tea. PETER tries to drink his tea. It is still
            disgusting.*

The cost to quality ratio in London is absolutely. Warped.

*DAISY is silent. PETER gets out a yellow NHS treatment consent form.*

Shall I read it out to you?

DAISY: Just sign it.

PETER: No, Daisy. This is just like any other contract or agreement. We need to Google this terminology so we're completely clear what we're signing up for. Get your phone out.

DAISY: I'll have to take my gloves off.

PETER: I can live with that.

DAISY: You'll have to have the tea back.

*PETER sighs and puts the tea on the floor whilst DAISY sorts herself out.*

PETER: Right. Cyclophosphamide. Shall I spell it?

DAISY: Yes.

PETER: C-Y-C-L-O-P-H-O-S-P-H-A-M-I-D-E

What does it say?

DAISY: It's loading.

PETER: –

DAISY: –

PETER: I thought these things were meant to be quick.

DAISY: Chemotherapy.

Which is what the Doctor said in there.

So we didn't need to Google it.

PETER: Daisy. I don't want to. And I'm trying very hard not to. But I'm going to get very angry with you in a minute.

DAISY:     And I'm going to get angry with *you* in a minute! Stop acting like I've got cancer and I'm going to die!

PETER:     Daisy –

DAISY:     I don't have cancer, Dad!

PETER:     No one's saying you do!

DAISY:     You're acting like I do! I mean. Is that what you want?

PETER:     Daisy. That is an absolutely disgusting thing to say! And if we weren't in public.

DAISY:     What? What would you do?

PETER:     Oh. I need a fucking cigarette!

DAISY:     What?!

PETER:     We need to talk this through. Today. Now.

DAISY:     You're going to start smoking?

PETER:     Daisy.

DAISY:     Don't you think that was a bit insensitive?

PETER:     It was a silly comment, Daisy.

DAISY:     Yes. It was.

PETER:     I'm sorry.

           But Mum didn't.

DAISY:     What?

PETER:     Smoke.

           Ok.

           Let's just calm down.

           Think practically for a moment.

           For instance, how are we going to get you down here and back every week.

DAISY:     The train.

PETER:    Yes obviously the train. Which is going to cost… Whatever it costs. Plus time off work.

        But that's all fine. That's ok. That's my problem. You don't need to worry about that.

DAISY:    I'm definitely going to go bald.

PETER:    Well. They said it was a low dose. Didn't they?

DAISY:    But what does that mean?

PETER:    It means you're *not* a cancer patient! I feel like a lightning bolt's going to strike every time we say that word. Like we're tempting fate.

        But, you know, Daisy this is what I mean about making sure you're clear on things. I mean, *why*… Why didn't you ask about the…your hair…when the doctor was talking to us?

DAISY:    I felt silly.

PETER:    Look. Let's be rational. Six weeks treatment to begin with. That's not that long.

DAISY:    I've already got bald spots underneath.

PETER:    What! Why didn't you tell me?

DAISY:    What are you going to do about it? Glue it back on?!

PETER:    You need to tell me if there are any changes!

DAISY:    So you can write it down?

PETER:    Yes!

        And I don't know why you're acting like that. Because me 'writing things down' has proved to not only be useful but very, very important, hasn't it?!

DAISY:    Whatever.

PETER:    You didn't ask about your hair. And, you know, you actually behaved not in the best way in front of that doctor. Did you? So if you want to talk about embarrassing, Daisy… And illogical.

DAISY:     Alright. Sorry! I just didn't like you handing over an A4 folder with my whole life in it!

PETER:     Your symptoms! I'm keeping a list of your symptoms so the doctors know what's been going on.

DAISY:     It was really embarrassing!

PETER:     I didn't know you would react like this!

DAISY:     Why didn't you tell me you were doing that?

PETER:     I don't know!

DAISY:     I will tell them what I want to tell them.

PETER:     Oh for God's sake. I wish you'd grow up.

DAISY:     –

PETER:     I'm trying to keep a grip on what's happening and it's very complicated Daisy.

Look. I don't want to fight with you.

I'm going to read it aloud. Ok?

You Google.

## FOUR

*DIANE's house.*

*Her old rotary dial telephone bleats three times with a loud and obnoxious brrring. DIANE is shocked by the sound. The phone never normally rings. She turns the television off but does not move.*

*The ringing stops. DIANE remains frozen. Just as she is about to turn the sound up the phone rings again. The phone rings off. Then it starts again, almost immediately. It rings persistently.*

## FIVE

*A café.*

PETER:     Thanks for coming.

DIANE:     Do you mind me keeping my coat on?

PETER:      It's ok.

DIANE:      I just feel a bit –

PETER:      Yes.

DIANE:      I'd prefer to just keep everything…on.

PETER:      It's fine with me. Absolutely. Go ahead. Do what
            you have to.

DIANE:      –

PETER:      I got you a tea.

            *DIANE nods but doesn't touch the tea cup.*

            How are you?

DIANE:      Alright.

PETER:      Diane. I.

            I really appreciate you turning up.

            I.

            This is difficult.

DIANE:      Are you getting married again?

PETER:      No.

            God. No.

            No, no.

            No. Categorically.

DIANE:      Oh. Ok.

PETER:      No. I, er, I want to talk about…something else
            altogether.

            *He passes her a leaflet. She takes it and put it on the table
            in front of her.*

            Um. Read it.

DIANE:      'Lupus: What is it?' *(Reads aloud.)*

PETER:      At your leisure. I meant. I meant read it later.

DIANE:      Oh. Ok.

PETER:      It just gives you the basics.

DIANE:      Thank you.

*PETER points at the leaflet.*

*DIANE looks down at the leaflet.*

PETER:      It's an auto-immune disease. So. The immune
system attacks itself.

DIANE:      Like. AIDS?

PETER:      No.

DIANE:      Sorry.

PETER:      You're not the first to have said that.

Anyway. The symptoms are very complicated.
There's a list in the leaflet. Um. Hair loss, sun
sensitivity, rashes. Then the bits you don't see.
Organ, er, damage.

DIANE:      Do you have it?

PETER:      No! It's Daisy.

DIANE:      Oh.

PETER:      Daisy has it.

*Beat.*

But… How are you?

DIANE:      Fine.

PETER:      Great.

DIANE:      Yes.

PETER:      All settled?

DIANE:      I've not moved house.

PETER:      No, I mean, you're happy?

DIANE:      I'm fine.

PETER:      Good. Good. That's good. What have you been up
to?

DIANE:      Bits and pieces.

PETER:      Working?

45

DIANE:      No.

PETER:      You must think I look like a fat old bastard these
            days, do you?

DIANE:      No.

PETER:      Sorry. I'm trying to say: 'It's great to see you
            again.' 'Time flies.' Something like that.

DIANE:      –

PETER:      You know *we* moved, right?

DIANE:      –

PETER:      Rebecca sent change of address cards. I think.

DIANE:      Yes. I have one.

PETER:      When Becky got ill I thought, 'fuck it', you know?
            'Life's too short and here's the proof.' So I spent
            a few days looking at various places, in various
            *villages* we'd always fancied living in. Now. It's
            nothing *flash* flash. Because even at the height
            of my madness I couldn't stretch to a thatched
            roof and an Aga. But there's a big double garage.
            In the new place. Seems odd calling it new
            because…well. We've obviously been there a while
            now. There's a nice garden. Room for parties,
            barbecues. But this double garage… The plan
            was to turn it into a pottery studio or artist's, er,
            whatever. It was the incentive. Because Becky had
            done this pottery class for a few months. But she
            hadn't had time to pursue it. And, you know, she'd
            really enjoyed it. So I thought…

            This is the long way round of telling you that I'm
            mortgaged up to the eyeballs. All for a garden
            I dread mowing and a big double garage that I
            shove boxes in.

DIANE:      Oh.

PETER:      And. You know my work is, er, project orientated?

DIANE:      No.

PETER:       Oh. Well. It is.

DIANE:       Right.

PETER:       I have to make sure they keep giving *me* the projects. And Daisy's appointments are always during the week between nine and five. Which has taken some juggling. And now she's about to start chemotherapy.

DIANE:       Why?

PETER:       Well because we're trying to avoid a kidney transplant. And the first step is to try a low dose of chemotherapy.

             If she needs my kidney in the end, I'll give her my kidney, you know. But. Well. I'm pretty attached to it. Ha ha.

DIANE:       Is it terminal?

PETER:       Doesn't have to be.

DIANE:       So it isn't.

PETER:       She's having treatment to make sure *it isn't*.

             It's all very positive. We're feeling very positive.

DIANE:       –

PETER:       It was worse before when we didn't know what was going on.

             She's just started going to this specialist clinic. In London.

             Central. On the river.

DIANE:       Oh.

PETER:       Opposite Big Ben. Lovely… Lovely location.

DIANE:       I've never been in here before.

PETER:       Shall I order you another tea?

DIANE:       No.

PETER:       Oh. No. You haven't drunk that one.

DIANE:  I haven't drunk this one.

PETER:  No.

Diane. The bottom line is Daisy needs to go to that clinic. But I can't jeopardize work. Because. There's just me.

I had a lot of time off to care for Rebecca. Used up…all savings. Professionally, it was a significant period of unreliability. I can't afford to do it again.

I didn't want to do it like this.

DIANE:  Don't you have any friends, Peter?

PETER:  I'm a bit favoured out. They say just to call but.

DIANE:  I thought you had a brother.

PETER:  He lives in Australia.

DIANE:  Oh. I didn't know that.

PETER:  You're the only person I can ask.

DIANE:  The last time you called me.

PETER:  I know.

DIANE:  I mean before you called me about this.

PETER:  I know. I only bring bad news.

DIANE:  Well. Yes.

PETER:  But we can think of it as an opportunity.

DIANE:  For what?

PETER:  I don't know. Just. An opportunity. For us all to get to know one another.

You're doing ok, you said.

DIANE:  I'm not able to, Peter.

I can't.

PETER:  Please.

## SIX

*PETER and DAISY's sitting room.*

PETER:     You should probably get ready.

DAISY:     Did you sleep in here?

PETER:     Why?

DAISY:     Answer the question.

PETER:     I drifted off.

DAISY:     You left the stereo on.

PETER:     No I didn't.

DAISY:     I thought you spent your life 'turning things off?'

Don't worry. I've done it.

PETER:     Breakfast.

DAISY:     No.

PETER:     Some toast. You need to take your pills.

DAISY:     I haven't forgotten.

PETER:     Please.

DAISY:     I don't want anything.

PETER:     It'd make me feel better.

DAISY:     Well. I'm not you.

PETER:     Here's some money. For a sandwich.

DAISY:     I don't have any pockets.

PETER:     Daisy. It means I can take time off at another point. If we need it.

DAISY:     Are you going straight into work?

PETER:     Once I've dropped you at the station, yes.

I've got to drive to Cambridge.

Here. For you.

*PETER hands DAISY a Clinton's bag. Inside is a pink mug saying 'Keep Calm and Carry On.'*

DAISY:     What's this?

PETER:     A mascot.

DAISY:     You've left the price on.

PETER:     It's a good luck mug.

DAISY:     Is this an idea you got from one of the books?

PETER:     Might have done.

           I'm trying, Daisy.

DAISY:     Is it a parenting book? From 'Sheree' in 'Birmingham.'

PETER:     No. It's from Amazon. I ordered it specifically to help *me* to help *you* in this situation.

           One of the many, many books on the subject I now own.

           Look it's…I thought it was funny. And it's pink.

DAISY:     I don't like pink anymore.

PETER:     –

DAISY:     You could just say you're sorry.

PETER:     I wish I could come today.

DAISY:     That's not what I mean.

PETER:     Daisy. I've explained.

DAISY:     I *mean* about the fact that you're abandoning me.

PETER:     You know it's not like that.

DAISY:     The *day* I start chemotherapy!

PETER:     I trust you to be mature about this.

DAISY:     Oh ok. Well. Thanks for the mug.

PETER:     She's your aunt.

DAISY:     First time I've met her though, isn't it?

PETER:     You met her when you were a baby.

DAISY:     What has that got to do with anything? How am I meant to remember that?

PETER:     It's one day. One day of your life. It's a trial. If
           it doesn't work out, then we'll think of another
           solution Go on. Get dressed.

DAISY:     You always said she was weird.

PETER:     No! I didn't! And you better be nice to her because
           –

DAISY:     Because what? She'll take me back to the
           gingerbread house if I'm not?

PETER:     She's not mental and it's going to be an adventure.

           She's also doing me – us – a massive favour
           because if I don't work then we're… We're fucked,
           alright?

## SEVEN

*DIANE's sitting room.*

*The telephone starts ringing.*

DIANE:     Hello?

           Yes.

           I'm. I'm fine.

           I'm ready. Ok.

           Twenty minutes.

           I'll look out for the car.

           Oh, what colour is it?

           Bye Peter. Bye.

           *DIANE hangs up.*

           It's important that I do this.

## EIGHT

*DIANE is on the bench outside the hospital. She is looking at Big Ben.*
*BOLA comes over. She has a large coat on.*

BOLA:      Hiya! Can I sit here?

Nice view isn't it?

It's cold but it's good to get some air.

DIANE: –

BOLA: You don't recognise me, do you?

*She opens hers jacket so that* DIANE *can see her uniform.*

I took your daughter's urine sample.

DIANE: –

BOLA: Hey. Do you mind if I smoke? It's not real. I'm giving up.

I like this bench. It's the best view in town.

I have my lunch out here in the summer. When I get my lunch.

*She lifts the cigarette.*

This is my lunch.

DIANE: –

BOLA: You look very alike.

DIANE: ?

BOLA: You and your daughter.

Same eyes or something.

Very pretty girl.

Ah. It is too freezing today! I don't get this place. Why is it cold? It's sunny out here.

DIANE: It's 'fresh.'

BOLA: What?

DIANE: My mother. Used to say that. When it was cold.

BOLA: Yeah. I can see that. I might use that. 'Fresh.'

A bit too fresh.

Where did you come in from today?

DIANE: Northampton.

BOLA: Ah! The North. I see. You're a northerner.

DIANE:      Not really…

BOLA:       That's why you're alright out here in the breeze!

DIANE:      Maybe.

BOLA:       You look so sad. You're worrying, worrying yourself sick! It's a lot to get your head around with all this nonsense. All the drugs and treatment. Sometimes it's good to talk to people who know, isn't it? Are you part of a support group up there in North?

DIANE:      I have a Community Care Liaison Worker.

            *Beat.*

BOLA:       Oh. No, sweetheart. I meant for your kid.

DIANE:      Oh.

BOLA:       So, your daughter's… What's her name again?

DIANE:      Daisy.

BOLA:       Well. I can give you some details. If you want.

DIANE:      It's. It's not really my decision.

BOLA:       Not for everyone. Bit share-y share-y. I like to keep my business to myself too.

DIANE:      This is my first trip to London.

BOLA:       Really?

DIANE:      I've only ever seen it on TV.

BOLA:       What?

DIANE:      Big Ben.

BOLA:       Really?

DIANE:      Yeah.

BOLA:       Ah! You make me feel bad. I just ignore it. It's just sort of there.

DIANE:      And parliament too.

| | |
|---|---|
| BOLA: | Oh! Don't worry about that. Load of crooks in there. Go on the London Eye. You can see *everything* on there. Get your money's worth. |
| | Now are you eating anything? |
| DIANE: | I'm fine. |
| BOLA: | Get yourself a coffee, a sandwich. Nurse's orders. It's too fresh and cold out here. |
| | It is a Marks and Spencer café inside. Very upmarket. |
| DIANE: | I don't know the way. |
| BOLA: | I am taking you with me! It is easy, I promise. It is right inside the door there. |
| DIANE: | – |
| BOLA: | Tell you what. If you get lost, I will come and save you. Like Super Mario. |
| | What's your name? Mrs… |
| DIANE: | Diane. |
| BOLA: | I'm Bola. |

## NINE

*PETER and DAISY's living room.*

| | |
|---|---|
| ALICE: | I didn't want to sit next to her. She asked me. |
| DAISY: | It's a free country, I suppose. |
| ALICE: | She's fallen out with slutty Ashley. So she was on her own too. |
| DAISY: | Oh dear. |
| ALICE: | It's only in French. |
| DAISY: | So. What does Vicky talk about then? How much of a bitch she *used* to be. |
| ALICE: | No. She talks about. Different things. |
| DAISY: | Like? |

ALICE:      Music.

DAISY:      And?

ALICE:      Fashion.

DAISY:      And.

ALICE:      Clubbing.

DAISY:      And.

ALICE:      I don't know. Stuff.

            Are you in a mood with me?

DAISY:      Do you laugh all the time with each other?

ALICE:      No. That's what you and I do.

            I am sorry Daisy.

DAISY:      What was she doing?

ALICE:      Who?

DAISY:      Who do you think?

ALICE:      Oh! Just sitting.

DAISY:      Ssh. Not so loud.

ALICE:      Sorry.

DAISY:      What was she doing though?

ALICE:      Well. I just went in and got the orange squash.

DAISY:      Yeah.

ALICE:      That's it really. She's just, like, sitting. In your
            kitchen.

DAISY:      I think *she thinks* she's got to hang out here like
            until Dad gets back.

            Fat bastard didn't even tell me his evil plan until
            *last night.*

ALICE:      Say what.

DAISY:      Yeah. Just roped her in as my fucking babysitter.

ALICE:      Oh well. Is she nice?

DAISY: You saw her. What does it matter? That is not the issue!

ALICE: I thought you had no family.

DAISY: I don't. Except for my Uncle Mike who lives in Australia.

ALICE: So. Is she the kind of aunt you only see at Christmas?

DAISY: I met her when I was baby. Apparently.

ALICE: That doesn't count.

Where's she from?

DAISY: *Here.* She lives in the town centre.

ALICE: And you *never* see her?

DAISY: Mum got upset when I asked about it. Dad said to ask Mum. Neither of them would talk about it properly so I stopped asking.

Oh. I don't care. Whatever. Families are weird.

ALICE: I don't know, Daisy. I've met everyone in *my* family.

Has she got any children?

DAISY: No.

ALICE: Husband?

DAISY: No.

ALICE: Job.

DAISY: No.

ALICE: Is the problem that she's a murderer?

*PETER enters from work.*

PETER: Hello Alice.

ALICE: Hi.

PETER: How are you?

ALICE: Er. Just dropping off some homework.

PETER:     Oh yes. Thank you. It's good of you to be so dedicated.

ALICE:     What?

PETER:     To Daisy's education.

ALICE/DAISY: –

PETER:     What has she got today?

ALICE:     Science. And Art.

DAISY:     We added them to the chart.

PETER:     Oh right, well Art doesn't matter so much.

DAISY:     It matters to me.

PETER:     Why didn't you text me?

DAISY:     What?

PETER:     After the treatment.

ALICE:     ?

DAISY:     I forgot.

PETER:     I don't think you did.

DAISY:     Do you mind not embarrassing me in front of Alice?

PETER:     Are you this rude to your parents?

ALICE:     Er.

PETER:     Hang on. Where's Diane?

DAISY:     In the kitchen.

PETER:     On her own?!

DAISY:     Yes.

PETER:     Daisy!

DAISY:     What?! Alice was waiting at the door when we got home.

           We came in here. Diane stayed in there. No one forced her.

PETER:     I'll run you home, Alice. Daisy's tired.

DAISY:      I feel fine.

PETER:      Another time. I need to take Diane home anyway.

DAISY:      Dad. The stuff was fine.

PETER:      I don't think it's a good idea.

DAISY:      The Stuff Was Fine.

PETER:      No.

DAISY:      We're going to stream *Twilight: Breaking Dawn* on Netflix!

PETER:      Another time.

DAISY:      Are you deaf? I Feel Fine.

PETER:      Alice understands, don't you?

DAISY:      We're watching. Fucking. *Twilight*.

PETER:      Daisy.

DAISY:      I promised.

PETER:      Alice understands.

ALICE:      It's alright, Daiz.

DAISY:      Fucking hell! Why are you always such a TWAT to me!

PETER:      THIN ICE, Daisy.

            *PETER exits to find DIANE.*

DAISY:      See what I mean? He's such a fucking wanker.

ALICE:      I've got something that'll cheer you up.

DAISY:      Go on.

ALICE:      So, Vicky and I went to Sainsbury's.

DAISY:      When?

ALICE:      The other day.

DAISY:      Why?

ALICE:      'Cause she was going and we were talking about it in Maths –

DAISY: Maths? I thought you just sat next to each other in French.

ALICE: Um. I wanted to see if they had any jobs going.

DAISY: What?!

ALICE: Hey. I've been thinking about getting a job at Sainsbury's for, like, time!

DAISY: But you've already got a job.

ALICE: Yeah but babysitting's shit. And if I get checkouts at Sainsbury's I'll get paid to sit down!

DAISY: You babysit. You get paid to sit down *and* watch TV!

ALICE: I hate children! All I wanted to tell you is that Kyle works in frozen food. So that if you're ever going down there, you put some make-up on and buy some alphabet shapes or something.

DAISY: Well thanks for cheering me up.

ALICE: Why are you being so mardy with me?

DAISY: I'm not. I just. Why is *everyone* getting jobs at Sainsbury's all of a sudden? I don't get everyone's obsession with Sainsbury's, that's all.

ALICE: It is a recession.

DAISY: What?

ALICE: A recession crisis.

DAISY: Alice. I don't think you understand what a recession is.

ALICE: Oh and you do? Suddenly you know like everything?

DAISY: Alright! Now who's being mardy!

ALICE: Sorry.

DAISY: You, my Dad. Is Diane just going to walk in here and have a go at me now?

ALICE: You just. You're really stressy.

DAISY: Well you're not very nice yourself at the moment, Alice. Must be Vicky rubbing off on you.

*PETER enters with DIANE.*

PETER: I'm going to take Diane back now.

DAISY: Ok.

PETER: You met Alice.

DIANE: –

PETER: No?

DIANE: –

PETER: Ok. This is Alice.

ALICE: Hi.

PETER: Thank you for today Diane.

DIANE: –

PETER: Daisy also wants to say thank you but I don't think she's feeling very well.

DAISY: For God's sake, I'm *fine*.

PETER: She means *thank you*.

DAISY: Yes! *Thank you*, Diane. Thank you *so much!*

PETER: Alice.

ALICE: Yeah?

PETER: Ready?

ALICE: Yeah.

DAISY: Bye Alice.

ALICE: Bye Daisy.

DAISY: I'm sorry. I'm really sorry.

ALICE: It's cool.

DAISY: Skype me.

ALICE: I will.

PETER: I'll be back in thirty minutes.

*ALICE and DIANE exit. PETER looks as if he wants to say something else.*

Hope you're proud of yourself, Daisy.

*He exits. The door slams.*

DAISY: FUCK YOU!

## TEN

*Two weeks later. DAISY and DIANE are on the train to London. DAISY holds a copy of 'Heat'. DIANE is holding a broadsheet newspaper.*

DAISY: Where are we?

DIANE: I don't know.

DAISY: Where was the last place we went through?

DIANE: The sign went too fast.

DAISY: What was the last stop you remember?

DIANE: I didn't look.

DAISY: They usually say it over the speaker.

DIANE: I didn't listen properly.

Sorry.

I'm sorry Daisy.

DAISY: It's ok.

DIANE: I won't miss the next one.

DAISY: It doesn't matter

DIANE: I'm very sorry.

DAISY: The train terminates at our stop. It's fine.

DIANE: –

DAISY: Really. It doesn't matter.

DIANE: Ok.

DAISY: I'm not saying that…stressy or anything. Ok?

Ok?

DIANE:     Yes. Ok.

           *DAISY applies suncream.*

DAISY:     Do I look mental?

DIANE:     What?

DAISY:     Is it rubbed in?

DIANE:     Yes.

DAISY:     It's winter, isn't it? People will think I'm a mental.

DIANE:     You don't look… You look. Cool.

DAISY:     I do not look cool, Diane.

DIANE:     I think you look cool.

DAISY:     Thanks. But I don't.

DIANE:     I like your glasses. I like your hat. Is it…a cat?

DAISY:     Yeah. I'm in disguise. It's hard for me to leave the
           house at the moment.

DIANE:     Me too.

DAISY:     Is that tea?

DIANE:     Yes.

DAISY:     With milk?

DIANE:     Yes.

           And sugar.

           Just one.

DAISY:     Loads of people are lactose intolerant and they
           don't even know.

           I'm switching to soya.

DIANE:     Are you allergic to milk?

DAISY:     Am I 'lactose intolerant' do you mean?

DIANE:     Yes.

DAISY:     Diane. It's nothing to do with lupus. I just read it in
           *Heat*.

           I'm going to try it out.

DIANE:      Lactose intolerance?

DAISY:      Soya.

            Something for me to do, isn't it?

DIANE:      I read the paper every day.

DAISY:      Dad's always trying to get me to read 'the paper.'

DIANE:      Do you want to read this?

DAISY:      Nah. Can't concentrate.

            Do you watch TV?

DIANE:      Yes.

DAISY:      I could sit a GCSE in ITV. *Jeremy Kyle. This Morning. Loose Women. Dickinson's Real Deal.*

DIANE:      I quite like *Midsomer Murders*.

DAISY:      Dad hates 'trash TV.' Everything's trash according to him. He won't get SKY, even for the football which he loves because the rest is 'trash.'

DIANE:      I don't have SKY. I don't even have Channel 5.

DAISY:      Well. If Dad got SKY, I could watch The History Channel. But. He won't.

            I like to read. But.

DIANE:      It's hard to concentrate?

DAISY:      Yeah. I don't even really watch TV properly to be honest. Just have it on. For company. So maybe Dad's right not to waste his money on SKY. Don't tell Dad I watch *Loose Women*. Or *Jeremy Kyle*.

DIANE:      I won't.

DAISY:      It'll just upset him.

DIANE:      Do you do crosswords?

DAISY:      Not in public. Do you?

DIANE:      Yes. I like to use my head.

DAISY:      You should get a brain-trainer.

DIANE:      What?

DAISY:      It's this… Never mind.

            Tell Dad we did a crossword. He'll love it. Might even get me a gold star in my homework chart.

DIANE:      –

DAISY:      You can read my *Heat*, if you like. There's a thing about Lady Gaga.

DIANE:      ?

DAISY:      Lady Gaga. Diane. Seriously.

DAISY:      I thought you said you read the paper every day.

DIANE:      I'm bad with names.

DAISY:      She wears…like dresses made of meat.

DIANE:      Oh. Oh yes. I remember that very clearly.

DAISY:      Bit mental. But. She's an artist.

            I don't like pop. But Lady Gaga's alright. She writes her own stuff.

            Means she's authentic.

DIANE:      I'll try and read it then.

DAISY:      Weird.

DIANE:      What?

DAISY:      No. I mean. You just had this expression that… Reminded me of her. For a split second.

DIANE:      We do look alike.

DAISY:      Did.

DIANE:      Do. I think about her every day.


## ELEVEN

*PETER and DAISY's sitting room. PETER is working on his laptop. DAISY enters eating a packet of crisps.*

DAISY:      You're back late. I was bored.

PETER:      Have you taken your pills?

DAISY:      This morning.

PETER:      Well. It's gone nine o'clock now. I hope you've also taken the second lot.

            *DAISY retrieves her pill pot, finds the right day and pours the contents into her hand. She puts them all into her mouth at once.*

            I find it very annoying when you do that.

            No. Don't shrug. I think I'm hoovering up more than you're actually taking.

            Don't laugh it's not funny.

DAISY:      It's a bit funny.

PETER:      No. It isn't. It's careless. And wasteful.

DAISY:      –

PETER:      How's it going with Auntie Diane?

DAISY:      Don't call her that.

PETER:      Why?

DAISY:      It doesn't suit her.

PETER:      Ok. How's it going with *Diane*?

DAISY:      I suppose.

PETER:      She's a nice lady.

DAISY:      Really.

PETER:      Sorry. Am I annoying you?

            I've spent the whole day at work dealing with arseholes in Abu Dhabi, Daisy.

DAISY:      Racist.

PETER:      Arseholes of all creeds, colours, nationalities in Britain *and* Abu Dhabi.

DAISY:      –

PETER:      I don't think it's, you know, much to ask.

            For some human contact. And stop eating that crap. It's bad for you.

DAISY:    –

PETER:    No Alice this week?

DAISY:    No.

PETER:    How come?

DAISY:    Mock exams, isn't it.

PETER:    What's that?

DAISY:    Mock exams.

PETER:    What?!

DAISY:    What?

PETER:    Why didn't you tell me?

DAISY:    Why would I tell you?

PETER:    Because I need to know, don't I? Because you're missing them, aren't you and it's important! For God's Sake.

DAISY:    Yeah, well, Alice hasn't been round so I forgot, didn't I!

PETER:    But you will have been texting each other!

DAISY:    No.

PETER:    Facebooking!

DAISY:    Not really. And I won't see her for ages now.

PETER:    I can't believe… Oh for God's sake, Peter.

DAISY:    She's going to Normandy after exams. The School Trip.

PETER:    Oh.

DAISY:    Remember.

PETER:    I remember that I haven't had the deposit back from the school yet.

DAISY:    Because that's all that matters.

PETER:    Do you want to go to bed? Because I don't have to put up with this.

DAISY:     Are you telling me to go to bed?

PETER:     No. Not yet. I'd like to hear about how it was today.

DAISY:     I don't want to talk about it.

PETER:     Ok. Fine. If you're going to be like that you can guess the next question. Did you do any schoolwork today?

DAISY:     Yes.

PETER:     What?

DAISY:     Some research.

PETER:     For what?

DAISY:     Art. My favourite subject.

PETER:     I know there's a lot going on, Daise, but I'm trying to… We've got to keep our eyes on the prize. Good GCSE results will make me and Mum proud. I know it's hard.

I'm not saying it's not hard.

But it's how the cookie crumbles, sweetheart.

*PETER sighs. Carries on tapping on the laptop.*

DAISY:     I drink this yellow stuff.

It tastes like sick.

That's what happens.

Yeah.

Tastes like… Like the nail stuff Mum put on my fingers to stop me biting them. But in a drink.

They hook me up. It's cold when it goes in.

They leave me magazines but I've already read them all.

The room I sit in is boring. The window looks out onto…nothing.

A courtyard. With nothing in it.

I can hear the staff. Talking.

Doors.

Whatever.

And Diane waits in the waiting room. I don't know what she does.

I just sit. And think.

Once it's finished. We sit in the clinic for half an hour in case anything bad happens.

Ok?

PETER:       –

DAISY:       But if you want to know how my kidney *feels*, whether it's *all better*, I haven't spoken to it recently because I can't see it and it doesn't talk.

PETER:       I just want to know you're ok.

DAISY:       I'm going to go to bed.

PETER:       Ok.

*DAISY exits to go to bed. She has just left when PETER says:*

I love you.


## TWELVE

*Outside St Thomas' Hospital. A bench facing Big Ben.*

BOLA:       I cooked egusi with pounded yam. 'Mummy, why are not eating?' And she looks like this and says 'There is no palm oil.' And I say 'Mummy, I have used palm oil!' 'There is no palm oil, jor? This thing that you have cooked here: I can only see that it is green and white! Palm oil is supposed to make the food red! And this is white and green!'

And I say 'Mummy, you tell me you like egusi. I cook egusi. There's palm oil, there's cow foot, there's goat meat, there's meat! There's everything you like!' She says 'I am now a liar! I am now a liar!' Then to my husband she says 'Adewale. She has pounded yam. How long did it take her to pound two yams?!'

This woman, this woman who does not read! Ah! My bride price was high for a reason. I have a good job. I have a BSc! You know? I don't have time for all this. Pounding yams. It is a process taking two and a half hours. Like…you know mashed potato?

DIANE:     Yes.

BOLA:     Pounding yams is like making mashed potato. But worse.

DIANE:     Oh.

BOLA:     And I don't always have time to make mashed potato from scratch for this ungrateful woman! I sometimes have to use a packet! I say to her, I say 'I work. Then I come home and I do every single thing. I wash, I cook, I clean. I have THREE children of my own to take care of. And you expect me to now come in from work and pound you yams. I thought you loved me more than this, Mummy!!'

And she says 'Oh city girl, not traditional' and turns to my husband and says 'Adewale. I can get you better wife. Get rid of this one.' This is what she says to him: 'I know a girl, Folashade, she has a PhD! Will wash children's clothes, will make pounded yam. When she cook, she will not cook this type of thing that is only green and white. No. I have not tasted it but I have eyes, I can see! There is no palm oil inside it! I am sorry for the people that are coming to eat here.'

And I'm trying to stay calm; 'Mummy, I do not want to disrespect my elders but…' And she screams 'Next WEEK! Next week FRIDAY I will go. In fact, if you want me to go tomorrow, I will go!'

NURSE: Is this your mother?

BOLA: No! God forbid! This is my mother-in-law! My mum knows when she comes and when she does not come! And I say to Adewale 'I have a mum too you know. She does not move in for three months.' And he says 'Why all this drama?!' and I say 'It is *not* drama. It is just the truth. Every time your mummy comes I smoke more, I sleep less, I put on weight.' Thank God for elasticated trousers! Makes me so mad. I get no peace when she is here.

DIANE: It sounds very difficult.

BOLA: My father said, he said to my husband, 'Tears must not fall from my daughter's eyes.' Eh. He should have said 'Listen boy she won't marry you unless you call your mummy to order.' But. Marriage is not a day's business. And when you marry, you marry the whole family.

DIANE: –

BOLA: Is your mother-in-law a troublemaker?

DIANE: No.

BOLA: Count your blessings, sweetheart.

## THIRTEEN

*PETER and DAISY's living room. There are some bowls of popcorn and a four pack of WKDs, two of which are open and are apparently being consumed. ALICE drinks hers throughout the scene.*

ALICE: Apparently they drink WKD for breakfast in Normandy. Tradition. Everyone just packs loads of alcohol in their bags and gets wasted in their dorms at night. My bag is literally massive. Don't know how I'm going to drag it to the coach tomorrow.

DAISY:     Oh. Yeah. Normandy. When do you go again?

ALICE:     Ha *ha*. Hiiiilarious, you joker.

           The men are fucking fit in France. Serious.

DAISY:     Yeah, well, send me a croissant or something.

           How is school?

ALICE:     Same.

DAISY:     It it *bof*?

ALICE:     Yeah. Basically.

DAISY:     Nothing's happened?

ALICE:     One funny thing happened the other day.

DAISY:     Yeah.

ALICE:     But I don't think you'll find it that funny. Can I smoke in here?

DAISY:     Um. Yeah. Ok. Dad's out.

ALICE:     Do you want one?

DAISY:     Er. What are they?

ALICE:     Benson and Hedges.

DAISY:     Oh. Um. Ok.

ALICE:     Do you have any matches?

DAISY:     Er. Somewhere.

           Actually, Alice. I can't really smoke.

ALICE:     Oh.

DAISY:     But you can. I don't care.

ALICE:     No. I won't if you won't.

DAISY:     Does Vicky smoke?

ALICE:     Mate. Vicky's proper hardcore. She's so addicted she wears Nicorette patches.

DAISY:     Is she still fallen out with slutty Ashley?

ALICE:     Oh. They're basically worst enemies now to be honest.

DAISY: I always thought slutty Ashley was the nicest one.

ALICE: Not when you get to know her. She's well up herself.

DAISY: Well, you know her now and everything.

ALICE: Ashley is a mega bitch. Seriously.

DAISY: Ok then.

ALICE: Let's just say that *a lot* of shit has gone down. It involves Marcus and his friend Ben. She's not going to be in *our* dormitory in Normandy. Trust. She's a dirty sket.

*ALICE receives a message.*

Ha. So funny.

DAISY: What is?

ALICE: Vicky just sent me a funny picture we took last week.

*ALICE shows DAISY her phone.*

DAISY: What's it like inside a club?

ALICE: Dunno. Like. Noisy.

DAISY: Where's this?

ALICE: Um.

DAISY: Was this taken in the loo?

ALICE: How did you know it was taken in the loo?

DAISY: You're leaning on the tampon machine.

ALICE: Oh. Well. I was wasted.

DAISY: So… Is this Fever?

ALICE: No.

DAISY: Well where is it?

ALICE: It's. Er. Just this place we went.

DAISY: So is it a club?

ALICE:      No. It's a bar. Or a pub. Whatever you want to call it.

DAISY:      Well. Which is it?

ALICE:      Look. I didn't get into Fever did I.

DAISY:      I thought Vicky sorted you fake ID.

ALICE:      Yeah but she bought it off the internet.

*ALICE passes the fake driving licence to DAISY. It's hilarious.*

The person in the photo has different hair.

DAISY:      Alice. They also have a totally different face.

ALICE:      I thought it wouldn't matter in the dark!

DAISY:      Who is this?

ALICE:      I dunno! It's some random off the internet, isn't it Daisy!?

DAISY:      How much did it cost?

ALICE:      Fifteen quid.

DAISY:      Woaaaah!

ALICE:      Do you want to hear the whole story or not? Give me that back.

DAISY:      Can I have it? This is classic.

ALICE:      Mate. I still have to use it till I can get a replacement.

*DAISY hands it back.*

Anyway. So I did manage to get into this place called The Bear.

DAISY:      Where is *that*?!

ALICE:      Does it matter?! It's in town!

DAISY:      Ok. Ok. Carry on.

ALICE:      It's an old-man pub.

DAISY:      What do you mean by 'old-man pub'?

ALICE:      It means… It means they don't care about ID in those sorts of places. Seriously, I was wankered at ten past eight. Probably had about twenty WKDs and five apple Sourz all told. There was a weird bit where some random man tried to grope Vicky. I sort of thought Marcus would step in. Or something. But all the boys just laughed so we went and hid in the loo for a bit. Vicky was quite upset actually. But then we went back and we were so wasted later on we forgot about it. Actually, I was sick in a plastic bag in the taxi home and Vicky took a photo because it was all blue and green. Honestly. Let me find it. You should see it. It's so funny.

DAISY:      Why did you drink that much?

ALICE:      Because that's what you *do* in town Daisy.

DAISY:      Alright. Easy.

ALICE:      I'm just saying: it's why you go. Everyone knows that. Children know that.

DAISY:      Can I ask you something?

ALICE:      Yeah.

DAISY:      It's important.

ALICE:      Go on then.

DAISY:      Don't talk to Vicky about me in Normandy.

ALICE:      I wouldn't talk to her about you. I'm not a bitch, Daisy. I know how you feel about her.

DAISY:      I just don't want…I don't want people to know stuff about me. Ok. I want to come back to school like none of this has ever happened.

ALICE:      Daisy.

DAISY:      What.

ALICE:      You have, like, missed so much work.

DAISY:      Why are you saying that?

ALICE: Because it's true.

DAISY: Well. I'm going to sit my exams in the summer.

ALICE: Why?

DAISY: Dad's got a meeting at the school.

ALICE: Exams are shit, if I could skip a year I would.

DAISY: But I don't want to skip a year Alice! I don't want to be left behind, ok?

   You have no idea how that feels.

ALICE: I don't get you sometimes, Daisy. I make so much effort.

DAISY: What's that supposed to mean?

ALICE: Nothing. I'm just saying. I try to like…include you.

DAISY: Include me?

ALICE: Yeah.

DAISY: –

ALICE: What are you looking like that for?

DAISY: Like what?

ALICE: Like *that*.

DAISY: You 'include' me.

ALICE: Yeah. I do. Not that you appreciate it.

DAISY: Didn't realise spending time with me was such a fucking chore, Alice.

ALICE: You're so selfish.

DAISY: What?

ALICE: I know you're ill and everything but you are.

DAISY: I'm selfish?

ALICE: You can be. Yes.

DAISY: Thanks.

ALICE: I come over here to see you and spend time with you.

DAISY:      Not much recently.

ALICE:      Dude. I have had mocks!

DAISY:      Anyway, I'm sure you'd rather be 'getting wasted' with Vicky.

ALICE:      Vicky's really nice actually!

DAISY:      She's not! She's a slag! We've *always* said what a slag she is!

ALICE:      You don't know anything about Vicky or her life or what she has been through.

DAISY:      And I don't care either! She doesn't know fuck all!

            She was so horrid about you in Year Seven, Alice. Don't you remember?

ALICE:      Daisy. We were eleven. I've got over it.

DAISY:      You said you wanted to kill yourself.

ALICE:      Pull it together, Daisy. I was eleven! What eleven year old goes and kills themselves?

DAISY:      I hate her. I'll never forgive her!

ALICE:      Daisy. You're. Not. There. Would you like me to walk around like a loner? Where's the crime in it.

DAISY:      She's a bitch and she'll just hurt you or spread rumours about you or…

ALICE:      She won't.

DAISY:      She will! I am loyal to you, Alice.

ALICE:      She won't because. She told me a secret.

DAISY:      What is it?

ALICE:      I can't tell you.

DAISY:      You're making it up.

ALICE:      Daisy. I'm really not.

DAISY:      Then tell me.

ALICE:      I can't. It's a big one.

DAISY: I don't see anyone! I don't even leave the house! Tell me!

ALICE: I can't.

*DAISY lifts up the WKD.*

DAISY: Have it back. I haven't drunk it.

I haven't drunk it because I can't drink.

Alice. Do you even know what a kidney is?

ALICE: Yes.

DAISY: What is it then?

ALICE: An organ in your body.

DAISY: But what does it *do*?

ALICE: –

DAISY: See. There's no point explaining anything to you.

ALICE: I can fucking *Google* what a kidney does.

DAISY: Well. I can probably never drink. Which seems to be the most important thing for you.

You and all your Sainsbury's friends.

ALICE: I don't even work in Sainsbury's yet!

DAISY: It's all you talk about!

ALICE: Daisy. Stop it. You're not thinking straight.

DAISY: Is it like watching an episode of some crappy soap for you, Alice?

ALICE: What's that supposed to mean? I don't know what to say to you! Whatever I do is wrong. I'm trying really hard.

DAISY: I can't be bothered with this.

ALICE: What are you saying Daisy? Say it to my face.

DAISY: –

ALICE: Fine. Fuck you.

*PETER comes home. He has been to the supermarket and is laden with bags.*

PETER: Oh. Hello, Alice.

ALICE: I'm just going home.

PETER: Oh. You don't have to.

ALICE: I do actually. I have somewhere to be.

*ALICE leaves.*

DAISY: Alice!

*Silence.*

PETER: Hi.

DAISY: Hi.

PETER: Oh my God. What the fuck is this? *(Picking up cigarettes.)*

DAISY: Oh, for God's sake!

PETER: What is going on here?! *(Picking up the WKD bottle.)*

What are you doing? Have you gone mad?

DAISY: Oh shut up!

PETER: What the hell are you doing drinking this blue shit and smoking fucking Benson and Hedges?! Daisy. You can't even be around smoke.

DAISY: You're not letting me explain!

PETER: You can't drink this stuff. What are you playing at!

DAISY: If you let me –

PETER: Answer me! Are you trying to kill me? This isn't a joke Daisy!

DAISY: Dad!

PETER: And Alice shouldn't be drinking either. I'm going to ring her mother!

*DAISY is hysterical. The house phone starts to ring.*

DAISY: Dad! Don't do that please! Please don't do that. I didn't drink it! I didn't drink it! I just held it!

I just held it! I just held it! I didn't even touch the cigarettes. Please. Alice didn't smoke. She doesn't smoke! I don't even know why she has them. Don't ring her mother. Don't embarrass me! Believe me, please. Please don't embarrass me. Please don't embarrass me!

PETER: Just. Just. Oh the fucking phone.

Hello?

Yes.

I said yes, it's Mr Briggs.

Can you slow down a bit?

No. I'm not interested, thanks.

You're clearly trying to sell me something. That's why I'm –

What?

Who said to call back?

You spoke to *my wife*?

Can I ask when?

Yesterday.

Oh. I see. You're a clairvoyant.

I said: are you a clairvoyant, do you have a crystal ball?

Well. Look. Let me level with you.

When you next speak to my wife – who died eighteen months ago, you lying little shit – you can ask her one or two things for me.

You can ask her where the house insurance policy is.

Ok? That would be good. I can't find it.

And then you can ask her why the fuck she wants another conservatory.

In that order.

Yeah, cheers, cheers.

Goodbye, you arsehole.

## FOURTEEN

*DIANE's house. DAISY is visiting for the first time. People don't normally visit DIANE.*

| | |
|---|---|
| DIANE: | You should sit down. |
| DAISY: | It's fine. |
| DIANE: | Please. |
| DAISY: | I'm just looking around. |
| | Why do you look so worried? |
| | I'm just tired. It's fine. |
| DIANE: | You're supposed to rest afterwards. |
| DAISY: | No infection or whatever can go wrong is going to make me feel any worse. Believe. |
| | It's weird. It's just like I remember it. |
| | Did you move in when Nan died? |
| DIANE: | Yes. She left it to me. |
| DAISY: | Where did you live before? |
| DIANE: | Different places. |
| DAISY: | Do you mind that I asked to come here? |
| DIANE: | No. |
| DAISY: | I didn't want to go straight home today. |
| DIANE: | It's nice to have a visitor. |
| | And. |
| | Anyway. |
| | I'm not…busy. |
| DAISY: | Lots of bits. |
| DIANE: | I get attached to things. |

DAISY: But. No photographs.

DIANE: No.

DAISY: I was hoping… Do you have any photos of Mum. From when she was a little girl? Ones that I might not have seen before?

DIANE: Probably somewhere.

DAISY: You know I'm really into art and stuff?

DIANE: No.

DAISY: Well. I am.

That's what I want to do with… My Life.

That's why I'm going to wear all, like, vintage clothes.

I mean. Not instantly. I don't have any money. Or a job.

I thought about looking through Mum's stuff.

But Dad put all her clothes up in the loft.

DIANE: –

DAISY: And. I don't want to ask him to get them down.

DIANE: I'm sure he would do it. If you ask.

DAISY: He'll say he will. But then won't.

I just want, like, a dress.

Something's that's really…cool. That no one else has.

Do you have any of Mum's clothes?

DIANE: I don't think so.

DAISY: Nothing?

DIANE: I keep things but. Mum and Dad. They would often chuck things out without telling us.

Me.

I don't know about Becky.

DAISY:     Becky.

DIANE:     Yes.

           Becky had a different…relationship with them.
           Maybe they kept her things. I'll look.

           Becky and I. We shared a bedroom. When we
           were little.

DAISY:     Did you?

DIANE:     Yes. Until I was fourteen.

           You can go in there if you like.

           It's not changed much.

           I don't go in there much.

DAISY:     Being my babysitter must be really boring for you.

DIANE:     No. Not at all.

           I love it.

           I'd never been to London before.

DAISY:     What, never?!

DIANE:     Not that I can remember.

DAISY:     That's so random.

DIANE:     Never had reason to go.

           I was very nervous. That first day.

DAISY:     Were you?

DIANE:     Terrified.

DAISY:     Of me?

           Feels like ages ago now doesn't it. It's only been a
           few weeks.

DIANE:     Have you ever been on the London Eye?

DAISY:     Yeah. When I was twelve.

DIANE:     Was it good?

DAISY:     I don't really remember. I was twelve.

DIANE:     You're only fifteen now.

DAISY:     Nearly sixteen.

DIANE:     I'm old.

DAISY:     No you're not.

DIANE:     Don't start telling me that you're old.

DAISY:     Ok. I won't.

DIANE:     What was it like on the London Eye?

DAISY:     I suppose it was…good.

DIANE:     Should we go on it one day?

DAISY:     Why not. It's next to the hospital.

DIANE:     I look at the London Eye. When you're… There's
           a bench. Where I like to sit. My bench. I always sit
           there. Look at the river. And Big Ben.

DAISY:     I like art galleries. They have good ones in
           London.

DIANE:     We could go to one of them too. I'd like that.

DAISY:     It'd be research for me.

DIANE:     ?

DAISY:     Because of what I just told you. About what I want
           to do with the rest of my life…

DIANE:     Oh. Yes.

DAISY:     Mum wanted to be an artist. Did you know that?

DIANE:     Your dad told me about the pottery class.

           And the double garage.

DAISY:     The double garage is the whole reason we moved
           house.

           She was supposed to, like, make her pots and get
           better.

           It was her 'incentive.' He used to use that word all
           the time.

           Dad's really good at 'coping', don't you think?

DIANE:     What do you mean?

| | |
|---|---|
| DAISY: | Coping – 'pretending everything is fine when it's totally shit.' |
| | I've fallen out with Alice. |
| DIANE: | Oh. |
| DAISY: | I'm pretty upset about it actually. |
| | I feel like shit. |
| | Sorry for swearing. |
| DIANE: | It's just not very ladylike. |
| DAISY: | No. |
| DIANE: | Why did you fall out? |
| DAISY: | I swear at Dad. More than I should. |
| | That first day. He gave me this disgusting pink mug. 'Keep Calm and Carry On.' |
| DIANE: | That's what you have to do. |
| DAISY: | Well. That's what it says on the front of the mug. 'Ha ha.' |
| | Don't be fooled. |
| DIANE: | By what? |
| DAISY: | By Dad. He's not coping. |
| DIANE: | How do you know? |
| DAISY: | I haven't seen Dad cry. Ever. But. He always falls asleep in the sitting room now. And I don't know why it bothers me…but it does. I think he just listens to music or watches TV or… Anyway. He's probably just going to have a heart attack and die or something. |
| DIANE: | That's not… |
| DAISY: | A very nice thing to say? |
| DIANE: | It isn't. |
| DAISY: | I was thirteen when Mum died. I was a lot nicer when I was thirteen. |

DIANE:    What do you mean?

DAISY:    I dunno. I was just nicer. I had more friends. I had more fun.

DIANE:    Happier.

DAISY:    Nicer. I didn't get cross about stuff or angry with people.

          Alice went to a foam party on Saturday. I saw it on Instagram. I don't really, like, use my Instagram anymore. Or Facebook. I don't know what to put in any of my statuses anymore. I should close it down but…then it'll be like I don't exist at all. Then again Dad is documenting my entire life.

DIANE:    What do you mean?

DAISY:    My symptoms.

DIANE:    Oh.

DAISY:    My homework. For the flipping homework chart. Well. I think I'm going to get chucked out of school so… In. His. Face. because that's all he seems to care about to be honest. That and money. Hates spending money. I try not to take any off him. Even when he offers it.

DIANE:    I think. I think it's good he writes your symptoms down.

DAISY:    It really pisses me off, Diane.

DIANE:    Why?

DAISY:    I can't explain. It's so fucking… It's weird. I mean, *why*? Why is he doing that?

DIANE:    Because he loves you, Daisy.

DAISY:    I know it makes sense. But.

DIANE:    It makes sense.

DAISY:    Sometimes *I* try and think back to when this all started. But I can't remember things…anything. And the doctors are always asking: 'When did you first start noticing blah blah blah.' But I can't remember. I really can't remember anything. Like. I cried at Mum's funeral. But I can't remember much about her being actually ill. I feel like. I feel like I don't remember much about *her* anymore. All I remember is just feeling tired. Just tired. And sad.

Why did you not come to her funeral Diane?

DIANE:      I wanted to.

DAISY:      I wish you had.

DIANE:      Daisy. I. I wanted to.


## FIFTEEN

*DAISY's school. PETER is late for an appointment with MISS LEWIS.*

PETER:           Hi.

MISS LEWIS: Hiya.

PETER:           I'm looking for Mrs Lewis.

MISS LEWIS: *Miss* Lewis.

PETER:           Oh right. Sorry. Don't tell.

MISS LEWIS: I won't have to. I'm Miss Lewis.

PETER:           Oh. Right. Oh my God I'm so sorry I'm late. The traffic was… And I'm really sorry for mucking you about on Tuesday too. Work's just… *(mental)*

MISS LEWIS: Are you Daisy's father?

PETER:           Yes! Sorry. Peter. Peter Briggs.

MISS LEWIS: So nice to put a name to the face!

Would you like some water or a cup of tea?

PETER:           No, I'm fine.

You're young for a headmistress.

I mean younger than expected.

             God. It was probably totally inappropriate that I said that, wasn't it?

MISS LEWIS: Ha. Well. I'm actually Deputy Head, so…

PETER: Oh. There we are then.

MISS LEWIS: But I also teach Daisy Maths. I don't *think* we met at parents evening…

PETER: No I couldn't make the last one. My wife used to do all of this, so I didn't have to think about it until…yeah.

MISS LEWIS: Well. I taught Daisy in Year Seven and then taken over from Mrs Jacobs this year because she's on maternity leave.

PETER: Ok. Cool.

MISS LEWIS: What I mean is: I taught Daisy before everything happened. How is she?

PETER: Alright. Travelling to London a lot to receive the, er, the treatment.

MISS LEWIS: How are you?

PETER: What?

MISS LEWIS: How are *you*?

PETER: I'm fine.

MISS LEWIS: We've had pupils with ME before which is similar to this…er, er, er.

PETER: Lupus.

MISS LEWIS: It was on the tip of my tongue.

PETER: I have a leaflet here. Saves confusion.

MISS LEWIS: Thank you. I think I have this one, actually.

PETER: Oh?

MISS LEWIS: Yes. This is the leaflet, you sent with your original letter, I think?

PETER: Oh. Sorry. Probably is.

MISS LEWIS: I'll take it anyway, shall I? To have it to hand.

PETER: She's having chemotherapy.

MISS LEWIS: I got that letter too.

PETER: Sorry. I forget what I've told people.

MISS LEWIS: Don't worry.

PETER: It is a low dose of chemotherapy.

MISS LEWIS: Stressful all the same.

PETER: Yes.

MISS LEWIS: For everyone.

PETER: Yes.

MISS LEWIS: Especially you. And if you're to-ing and fro-ing from London…

PETER: My, er, my sister-in-law is lending me a hand.

Just got to hope it works. Because. If it doesn't.

Anyway.

Alice has been bringing Daisy her homework.

MISS LEWIS: Alice Adams?

PETER: Yes.

MISS LEWIS: Oh. That's…nice of her.

PETER: Yes. I've been keeping a chart of what's come in when.

MISS LEWIS: Good. That's really good to hear.

PETER: And Daisy's been looking through it. A bit. When she's been. She's often in a lot of pain. Um. I think I know what you're about to say to me.

MISS LEWIS: Do you?

PETER: Yes. I know she's missed the mocks. I just don't want you to think I've been, er, slacking.

MISS LEWIS: I don't think that, Mr Briggs.

PETER: Ok.

MISS LEWIS: From our perspective, we've been letting things float until you knew what was happening. But obviously it's now reached a stage where she has missed a lot of school. So. We have to start talking now about how we move forward.

PETER: Ok.

MISS LEWIS: Because this is an important academic year.

PETER: Yes.

MISS LEWIS: And Daisy is one of our more able students.

PETER: She. She's a clever girl.

MISS LEWIS: And so we think… And I want you to know that I, personally, think this too. We think it would be an idea for Daisy to repeat this year. And there's absolutely no shame in that.

PETER: Ok.

MISS LEWIS: It's in her best interests academically. It's not a punishment.

PETER: I just.

We, Becky and I… It's not like we're those parents who say 'right, she *will* be Prime Minister' but it mattered to me that she went to University, if she wanted to and if she was capable. And if she wasn't that was fine. But she is. And. I just…

I've bought all the revision guides. I have…this chart. With all her homework on it. I want her to keep focused. On something. Something that's worth it. I want her to have goals.

If there's no schoolwork, I find it quite hard to know what those goals should be. If there's no schoolwork, I don't know what to do. I don't know what to do at all.

MISS LEWIS: Stop beating yourself up. That's the first thing you should do.

PETER: –

MISS LEWIS: I don't know how you're coping, quite frankly. But you are. And it sounds like you're doing a great job.

PETER: –

MISS LEWIS: Right, Mr Briggs. This is what we're going to do. You're going to keep her chipping away at stuff for the time being. Carry on with those revision guides, they'll have the complete syllabus.

PETER: Ok.

MISS LEWIS: Now. Alice Adams is…lovely. But I think we maybe need a better long-term strategy in place. That'll require some planning. So leave that with me and I'll give you a call once I've spoken to some of the other teachers.

PETER: And…the revision guides won't go out of date?

MISS LEWIS: No! Even Michael Gove isn't going to be able to change the fundamentals.

PETER: Yes. Oh. They're all tossers in the end, aren't they?

MISS LEWIS: Well.

PETER: Sorry.

Thank you.

MISS LEWIS: No problem.

PETER: And.

Thank you for asking how I am.

I think it's because I'm the adult in the situation.

No one has asked me yet.

MISS LEWIS: Take care of yourself.


## SIXTEEN

*Outside St Thomas' Hospital. A bench facing Big Ben.*

DIANE: Hello Bola.

BOLA: The sun has got his hat on!

DIANE:  What?

BOLA:  There is sun today.

DIANE:  Oh. Yes.

Has she gone?

BOLA:  Who?

DIANE:  Your mother-in-law.

BOLA:  Oh! Yes. Thank God. And I'm still not smoking.

DIANE:  Well done.

BOLA:  You're not a smoker are you…?

DIANE:  No.

I. I had a boyfriend who used to give me cigarettes. Stuart. He was quite a lot older than me.

BOLA:  Oh. The older man.

DIANE:  He was thirty. I was fourteen. Looked old for my age. Didn't really know…what I was doing.

BOLA:  Oh. That's. That's very interesting.

Has your daughter got a boyfriend?

DIANE:  I don't know. We don't talk about…that.

BOLA:  It can all be a bit awkward.

DIANE:  I'm not…I'm not Daisy's mother.

BOLA:  Oh. Oh right.

DIANE:  I'm her aunt.

BOLA:  I see.

DIANE:  Peter, her dad, asked me to take her to London. To help him out.

And it was…it was very strange that he asked me because I hadn't seen him for fifteen years.

BOLA:  What? Really?!

DIANE:  The last time I saw him…it was with Becky, my sister. Becky is Daisy's mother. They came to visit me when Daisy…when Daisy was born. I was in a hospital. Not like this one. This one is very nice. They asked me if I wanted to hold…to hold her. I didn't say anything, I don't think. I should have said no. I really wasn't…myself. I was very… Distressed.

And. I don't remember but…I'm lying. I do remember. I remember thinking that I was going to scream. Because this perfect, perfect baby wasn't mine.

Becky died. Not very long ago. But I didn't go to the funeral because…because I wasn't brave enough. And. I feel…I feel truly awful about it. Because she was my little sister and I loved her.

And I wanted your opinion. On whether I should tell Daisy.

BOLA: What?

DIANE: What I've just said.

BOLA: Er.

DIANE: And. The other things that I haven't.

Because I'm not a mother and. You are. You have three children, you said.

BOLA: Well. I don't know all the details.

DIANE: I'm sorry to ask.

BOLA: No. It's. It's ok.

Er. I mean I don't know all the details *but,* as a parent, it's a big compliment for Mr Briggs to trust you to help him. Big compliment.

But. I don't know whether you need to tell her all this stuff you tell me. It is in the past, isn't it?

DIANE: Yes.

| | |
|---|---|
| BOLA: | The past is the past. It doesn't matter. Tell her…<br>Tell her when the time is right. When everything is less busy. |
| | That is just my opinion. |
| DIANE: | Thanks. Thank you. |
| BOLA: | Hey. So you're Daisy's auntie? Hello auntie. |
| DIANE: | Hello. |
| BOLA: | We know where we are standing now, sweetheart. |
| DIANE: | Yes. |
| BOLA: | Stop worrying. |

## SEVENTEEN

*The remnants of a makeshift birthday party in* PETER *and* DAISY's *sitting room. The table is laden with takeaway boxes. A cake box. Half of a big bottle of Pepsi.*

| | |
|---|---|
| PETER: | So. A toast? |
| | *PETER raises his glass. So does* DIANE. DAISY *lifts hers. A bit.* |
| | My compliments to Mr Wok of The Wok Inn for the main course. |
| | I can already feel my arteries seizing up. |
| | Did you enjoy your meal, Diane? |
| DIANE: | Oh yes. I did. I would eat Chinese again. |
| PETER: | Oh great. Well. Good. Anyway. This day. Sixteen years ago. I was doing a crossword because Rebecca had been in labour for approximately three days. At thirty-three she was worried she would never have a baby. At thirty-four, she was demolishing several cans of gas and air. She turned to me and said: 'Actually, after all this, you'll have to love this child. Because I don't think I can.' And I said. 'Well. Ok.' And that is what I have done for sixteen years. And what my beautiful wife did for |

thirteen. With all her heart. Because the second she held you in her arms, Daisy –

DAISY: Alright, Dad.

PETER: To absent friends. Or should I say. Absent friend.

Hurrah: The big one six.

DIANE: Do you feel different?

DAISY: I don't know.

PETER: Sixteen and no different?

DAISY: No.

PETER: Oh well.

DAISY: 'Oh well.'

PETER: Diane. You may have noticed that Daisy and I are not talking.

DIANE: I've got. I've got this. Sorry about the paper. 'Happy Christmas.'

PETER: Ooh. Very good Diane.

*DAISY opens the parcel. There is a photograph on the top. DAISY looks at it for a long time.*

Is this Mum?

DIANE: Yes.

DAISY: I've never seen this one before.

DIANE: I can't remember but…I think. I think we were camping. My father's cousin liked to sew. And she always made two of everything for Becky and me. Matching. I hated it. Felt I was too grown up to wear the same thing as my baby sister.

*DAISY opens the dress out. It is a sleeveless shift in indigo, white and blue. It has a large butterfly print.*

I only wore it that once. I was in the hospital not long after this was taken. And I had put on a lot of weight by the time I came out. So it's brand new.

DAISY: No it's not. It's vintage.

DIANE:    Oh. Yes. Vintage.

DAISY:    Wait. One minute.

          *DAISY exits.*

DIANE:    It's very special to be at this party. Thank you for inviting me.

PETER:    Well. She seems very pleased. Well done you.

DIANE:    She wanted something of Rebecca's to wear.

PETER:    Fashion goes over my head.

DIANE:    Are you alright, Peter?

PETER:    Yeah. Why.

DIANE:    –

PETER:    I'm just the guy who works and worries.

DIANE:    Daisy and Alice have fallen out.

PETER:    I had noticed she hasn't been around for a while.

DIANE:    Daisy says they're not even talking on Facebook.

PETER:    Oh. Oh well.

DIANE:    They haven't spoken. For weeks.

PETER:    They're thick as thieves. They'll get over it.

DIANE:    I don't know if they will.

PETER:    They're teenage girls. They fall out all the time. It's their job.

DIANE:    It's different.

PETER:    Don't waste your energy on Daisy's melodrama, Diane. She's famous for it.

          *He checks.*

          She's not taken her pills.

DIANE:    What?

PETER:    Every fucking day. I say it every fucking day. I say it so much, I bore *myself*, Diane.

          *DAISY re-enters. She does a turn.*

DAISY:      I love it, Diane. I love it so much.

PETER:      Very nice. You haven't taken your pills.

DAISY:      I'll take them now.

PETER:      Yes. You bloody will.

            *DAISY puts them all in her mouth at once.*

            You're a little prat sometimes. Do you know that?

DAISY:      Maybe that's because you're a big prat.

PETER:      Do you want to know why I'm being punished, Diane?

DAISY:      Stop it, Dad.

PETER:      No. Shut up, Daisy. I'm talking. Diane, today I had the nerve to suggest that we go out in the car for a drive.

DAISY:      No. You said you needed to go to B&Q and I should come out for the drive. Right after you bollocked me for not being dressed.

PETER:      I needed to buy some wood stain.

DAISY:      I don't want to watch you buy wood stain.

PETER:      But Daisy I needed to buy wood stain. I needed to paint the fence. Something you don't seem to understand is that if I don't do it no one will. And the end of the story is, Diane, that I went out and bought the wood stain. And then I painted the fence. And did all the other essential tasks on my list today. Meanwhile, Daisy did whatever she did all day long. Nothing useful, I'm sure –

DAISY:      Dad. Stop it.

PETER:      But one thing she certainly did *not* do is take her pills. Anyway, whilst I was out there, painting the fence, thinking about the day she was born, thinking about her first steps, thinking about how much I love her, how much I sacrifice for her; my mind drifted to Rebecca. And then I started thinking 'How did this become my life?' I thought about how scared I am about the future and how fucking lonely I am. I started worrying about what would happen to Daisy if I were to die. And then. And then I thought about the opposite. I thought about the fact that I might have years and years to live through. By myself.

Now, Daisy. Why. *Why* did you not take your pills?

*Silence.*

DAISY: Because it's my sixteenth birthday, Dad.

PETER: And we're having this party in your honour, Daisy.

DAISY: I wanted to go to the V&A! Ok. That's what I would have liked to do!

PETER: I don't know what you're talking about.

DAISY: The V&A, Dad! It's a really famous museum!

The V and A, Dad! Not The B and Q.

PETER: Grow up.

DAISY: I wanted to be well enough –

PETER: Yes? So take your pills.

DAISY: I wanted to do something she would have liked!

PETER: Here we go.

DAISY: And *she* wanted to be an artist.

PETER: She did a night class in pottery!

DAISY: Exactly!

PETER: She liked to go to galleries. *Sometimes*!

DAISY: So! What's your point?

PETER: She would never have given up her job to be a bloody 'artist'!

DAISY: Then why did we move to this stupid house?!

PETER: I wish you would get over this fantasy you have about her. Like. Like. Like, ok. Like I'm some shithead ruining your life when actually, *actually* Daisy Briggs, I am all you've got and I'm working my balls off to keep this house together!

DAISY: Fuck you.

PETER: Do not use that kind of language to me!

What are you? A. A. A fishwife?! Do you want people to think you are a fishwife, Daisy?

DAISY: Listen to yourself.

PETER: Listen to *yourself.*

DAISY: You know nothing!

PETER: No. *You* know nothing. *You* know nothing. You are an extremely *privileged* young woman, Daisy. You're letting your mother down to behave this way. And since you're incapable of thinking of me, why don't you try thinking of her. What would she think of your behaviour at the moment? I can't stand your selfishness!

DAISY: *My selfishness?* Just fuck off and die and leave me then, you fool.

PETER: Do you think the world owes you a living? Do you?

DAISY: The world doesn't but you do! I'm your daughter!

PETER: I am *reading* the leaflets. I am *reading* the books. I have practically bankrupted myself buying every fucking thing I can lay my hands on off Amazon. The Parcel Force vans are gridlocked up the street! But I am one man Daisy! I am ONE. MAN.

DAISY: *I* am the one living with it, Dad! ME! It's nothing to do with YOU! Half the time you won't shut up about it. Half the time you act like I'm just lazy and don't believe me! What do you want?!

PETER: I want you to take your pills when you're supposed to! I want you to do your homework! And I want you to get dressed every day – whether you feel like it or not! I'm breaking here, Daisy. I'm trying so hard. I am trying so hard. I need some help! I need something in my life that isn't stressful!

DAISY: What are you talking about?

PETER: DAISY. I need you TO BE NORMAL.

I *need* it. I *need it*.

BE NORMAL.

DAISY: Shut up! SHUT UP! Shut up, YOU CHUMP!

PETER: BE NORMAL! BE NORMAL! THIS IS NOT HOW IT TURNS OUT!

DAISY: I CAN'T BE NORMAL ANYMORE!!!!

PETER: BE NORMAL. BE NORMAL. BE NORMAL. BE NORMAL. BE NORMAL.

*PETER continues to shout. He puts on the CD player. The loudest, happiest music blares out and he starts dancing around. DAISY storms out. PETER sits on the sofa.*

*DIANE turns the music off. She sits with him in silence for a long time.*

PETER: I keep thinking about what happens if this gets worse.

I don't think I'll be able to cope.

DIANE: What do you mean?

PETER: What if.

What if this chemo doesn't work?

What if.

She needs a donor.

And I'm not a match.

DIANE: Peter.

PETER: If I'm not a match for Daisy. We're going to have to go on a list. I'll be sitting here wishing, hoping, praying for some other sod to die, won't I? Who else can I ask?

DIANE: Peter.

PETER: I don't want her to end up on dialysis, Diane. I don't want this for her. And I don't know how to protect her and I don't know how to save the day. And it's breaking my heart.

I have realised something so important.

I have realised that what I want most of all is for Daisy's life to be.

Just.

Uncomplicated.

An uncomplicated life.

What a gift.

DIANE: Why did you ask me to help with Daisy, Peter?

PETER: Because there was no one else.

DIANE: –

I just thought. I'll meet for a coffee. And see how it goes.

I don't have to ask her anything.

I just sort of bluffed it.

But, in the end, I did ask you. Because I knew it would be ok. And it has been ok. Hasn't it?

DIANE: –

PETER: And I've been meaning to say, Diane.

I don't know what happened… But I'm just sorry for all the wasted time.

I think Rebecca would be really, really pleased.

And I think she would be really proud of you.

And I hope you forgive her – us – for any mistakes we made along the way in the past too.

DIANE: Peter?

PETER: Yes.

DIANE:    This. This has been the best thing that has happened to me.

PETER:    –

DIANE:    And I want you to ask me.

PETER:    What?

DIANE:    Ask me what you need to ask me.


## EIGHTEEN

*PETER and DAISY's sitting room. ALICE has come round.*

ALICE:    So. What else have you been up to?

DAISY:    Not a lot. Just. Appointments.

ALICE:    When are you coming back?

DAISY:    I'm skipping the year now. For definite.

ALICE:    Will you be back in September?

DAISY:    Dunno.

DAISY:    Normandy looked fun.

ALICE:    Oh.

DAISY:    I saw. On Instagram.

ALICE:    It was alright

DAISY:    And you went to a foam party.

          I saw on Facebook.

ALICE:    Yeah. They're funny. There's just, like, loads of foam.

DAISY:    And music.

ALICE:    Yeah. Drink, music, bit of dancing.

DAISY:    Cool.

ALICE:    How's it going with the freak?

DAISY:    What?

ALICE:    Your 'Aunt.'

DAISY:     Don't say that Alice.

ALICE:     Sorry.

DAISY:     No. I'm sorry. I feel guilty about what I said about her before. She's actually really nice. She gave me this.

ALICE:     I was going to say. It's really cool.

DAISY:     Yeah.

ALICE:     Is it vintage?

DAISY:     Yeah.

ALICE:     I didn't forget.

*ALICE hands DAISY a birthday card.*

           Are you going to have a party?

DAISY:     Had it.

ALICE:     Oh.

DAISY:     Just Dad and Diane. A takeaway. A cake from a petrol station with a Marks and Spencer. A really bad argument. You didn't miss anything.

ALICE:     What happened?

DAISY:     Doesn't matter. Tell me something funny.

ALICE:     I don't know what to tell you.

DAISY:     How's Vicky?

ALICE:     She's good. New boyfriend.

DAISY:     Is she friends with Gemma F again?

ALICE:     Yeah. I do have some not so great news.

DAISY:     Great. What is it?

ALICE:     I found out that Kyle has a girlfriend.

DAISY:     Oh.

ALICE:     Yeah. They've been going out for two years or something. So he loves her and shit.

DAISY:    That's fine. I don't even know him, do I? It's not like he's cheating. And I would never have been brave enough to add him on Facebook. I am glad we found out his surname though.

You haven't spoken to me in a month.

ALICE:    You haven't spoken to *me*.

DAISY:    I figured you didn't want to.

ALICE:    I figured *you* didn't want to. Like. You needed space. I don't know.

DAISY:    We've… Haven't we.

ALICE:    What?

DAISY:    We said it would never happen.

ALICE:    It hasn't.

DAISY:    It has.

ALICE:    It hasn't.

DAISY:    We've drifted.

ALICE:    All this stuff has happened to you. And I'm frightened. And I feel like I'm getting everything wrong because I don't…I don't understand. I know I don't understand. I don't know…I don't know what to say. I can only say: I'm really sorry it's all shit, Daisy. And I am. I'm really sorry.

Do you remember…when your dad came to pick you up from my house. When he came to tell you that your Mum had…gone.

DAISY:    You've been a really good friend to me, Alice.

ALICE:    No. I don't mean that…I mean. We share that. We're more than wifeys. We're like…family.

DAISY:    I don't understand what's happening. I mean. I just try not to think about it. But I can't help it. Am I going to die a virgin, Alice? Am I going to get married? Will I give my children this? Can I even have children. And I'm literally going bald. A chunk of hair was on the pillow this morning.

I didn't tell you. But I'm having chemotherapy.

ALICE: Why didn't you tell me?!

DAISY: I didn't want you to think I had cancer.

ALICE: What?

DAISY: I don't have cancer, Alice.

ALICE: Ok. Um. I thought it was your kidney.

DAISY: It is. It's complicated.

ALICE: Phew. Ok. Open your card.

*DAISY opens it.*

Yeah. It's supposed to be a kidney. A glittery one. With a smiley face.

DAISY: Oh.

ALICE: I Googled it.

DAISY: I miss you so much, Alice.

ALICE: Daisy. I love you. Not in a gay way.

DAISY: I love you too.